Talking about Symphonies

ANTONY HOPKINS

Talking about
SYMPHONIES

an analytical study of
a number of well-known symphonies
from Haydn to the present day

WADSWORTH PUBLISHING COMPANY INC.

BELMONT, CALIFORNIA

Printed in Great Britain

TO ROGER FISKE
IN GRATITUDE

ILLUSTRATIONS

The diagrams and musical examples
have been drawn by John Barkwith.

CONTENTS

KNOWING THE FORM

NOBODY CAN EXPECT to enjoy listening to a symphony to the full unless he has at least a basic knowledge of what symphonic form means. Such music is conceived by the composer in an almost entirely intellectual way; it is neither 'mood' music nor 'programme' music. One might say that the first movement of a symphony, in particular, is to music what the thesis or monograph is to literature; in it the composer selects certain musical materials, usually of a concise nature, and explores their potentialities to the limit; they can be developed both physically and emotionally—physically by extending their length, changing their rhythmic shape or by any one of a number of techniques, emotionally by altering the mood which they originally suggested. Perhaps the hardest thing for the untrained ear to grasp is what might be termed the architectural aspects of a major composition. (Musicologists have coined the word 'architectonic' to describe these, but this strikes me as being technical jargon of a rather forbidding kind.) The reason for the uninitiated listener's difficulty is quite easy to trace; it is a matter of recognition and memory, of being able to store music in the mind and instantly to recognize derivations and extensions.

To a composer it is vital that you should be able to compare what happens on page one of a symphony with some later moment, say page forty-one. At this point he may make some miraculous twist, turning the music in a totally unexpected direction, thereby revealing some new and unsuspected facet. If the listener is merely conscious of the immediate sounds that are audible at any given moment, he will miss the whole purpose of such a passage; he might just as well listen to a nocturne or a waltz, a type of music which is only concerned with establishing a mood. Such pieces are the equivalent of the short poem or literary vignette; the whole intention of a symphony is to explore the innermost possibilities of its material, and to make its themes grow and proliferate. What such 'development' means we can investigate in greater detail at a later time;[1] for the moment, let us have a quick look at the basic form which embraces most symphonies. The textbooks call it Sonata Form, though it is common to many types of composition, including sonatas, trios, quartets, symphonies and, in a somewhat modified guise, concertos.

If you take a tune like 'The Bluebells of Scotland' you will find that it consists of a first phrase, which is immediately repeated, then a rather different melodic shape, followed by a final repetition of the opening. Not to get too technical about it, you could describe it as A A B A. Now this extremely simple and fundamental musical shape is so profoundly satisfying in its logic and symmetry that it is capable of very considerable elaboration. It is in fact the foundation on which sonata form has been built; one does not have to be a mathematician to be able to see a parallel between these two formulae.

(i)	A	A	B	A
(ii)	Exposition	Exposition repeated	Development	Exposition repeated again

The reason for the repetitions of the first section, or *exposition* we shall see in a moment; meantime, a third technical term must be learnt and that is the *recapitulation*, which is what musicians call the fourth section of the formula above instead of the rather clumsy 'exposition repeated again' which I have used. In fact, even to suggest that this fourth section is a mere repetition is dangerous; one of the biggest misunderstandings of the dramatic potentialities of the sonata springs from this too easy generalization. But then the textbook definition of sonata form can scarcely be said to be illuminating; too often, the most exciting and fruitful shape that composers have ever devised is reduced to this chillingly academic verbiage.

[1] See pp. 14–17.

Sonata-form, which is normally applicable to first movements only, consists of three main sections, the Exposition, Development, and Recapitulation; the Exposition begins with the first subject in the tonic key which is joined by a modulatory bridge passage to the contrasting second subject, which may usually be expected to appear in the dominant; this section is rounded off with a codetta which finalizes the newly established key, and by tradition the whole exposition is repeated. In the Development section which follows, the composer amplifies, extends, and explores the potentialities of the material presented in the Exposition; the Recapitulation re-states the material in its original form, but with a modified and non-modulatory bridge passage so that the second subject is now in the tonic, thus confirming the tonality of the movement.

How infinitely unlovable such definitions make music sound! It is like a botanist who reduces flowers to stamens and pistils but cannot appreciate the beauty of a bed of roses. What is worse is the inflexibility of such a formula; few sonatas would fit into this rigid mould, for curiously enough, it is impossible to say with any certainty how this extraordinarily fruitful form actually materialized. There was no composers' conference at Margate in 1773 at which sonata form was finally ratified; like Topsy in *Uncle Tom's Cabin*, it just grew, and its consequent freedom from academic restraint is one of its greatest glories.

The fairest comparison I can think of is to regard the first movement of a sonata as one would regard a house. We all understand the function of a house, and we appreciate the infinite variety that this generic term can encompass. There are small houses and great houses, houses with two rooms or a hundred rooms, one floor or six; so do sonatas and symphonies vary, and to compare an early Haydn symphony with Sibelius's seventh, or a Scarlatti sonata with Liszt's great piano sonata in B minor is like comparing an attractive cottage to Blenheim Palace. To pursue this comparison in greater detail will shed a good deal of light on the forbidding definition of sonata form which is printed above. Let us start with a basic house—what a county council would be entirely justified in calling a 'dwelling-unit'.

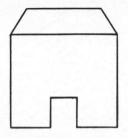

As you see, it has a front door, and a number of sonatas and symphonies also have front doors; the first page of the Pathétique Sonata of Beethoven is nothing but an imposing entrance, as are the slow introductions to his first and second symphonies. A composer may or may not have such an introduction at will; it is a matter for his personal taste entirely. As a general rule, however, the earlier symphonies are more likely to have a slow introduction, since the symphony was originally derived from the orchestral suite; such suites tended to begin with grave and solemn dances, and reserved the quicker movements like the gigue (or jig) to the end. The parallel between this and the joyful finale of a symphony is too obvious to need underlining. Having examined the front door, having experienced the introduction to the movement proper, let us continue our exploration of this particular house.

When you go inside a house, all sorts of architectural possibilities are available; you may find a hall, with several doors opening off it into different rooms; or you may find one immense room with a staircase leading directly from it. The same thing applies to the sonata or symphony; it can have one, two, three or more contrasting ideas, or one big theme, or a mixture of large-scale melody and small concentrated patterns. The so-called 'first subject' is seldom one tune; it usually consists of a group of themes, often brief in themselves but adding up to a total conception of unity, just as the downstairs part of a house is a unit, even though it may have several rooms. In order to go upstairs and find those rooms that are designed for the other functions of living we must use the staircase, and this in musical terms is known as the bridge passage. It leads us from one mood to another, from one set of themes to another; even more important, it leads us from one 'key' to another. Just what this means we shall see later on (pages 18–22), but for the moment let us continue our exploration of the house.

Once upstairs, we find contrasting rooms, and again they may be any shape, size or number; we called the downstairs part the first subject, and as you might expect, the upstairs part represents the second subject. Of the two, this is the more likely to be a lyrical sustained melody, since its emotional function is usually to be a foil to the first subject material, which, in order to arrest our attention, naturally tends to be positive and rhythmically alive. To round off our house we have an attic—not the most exciting room in the building, and musically this is represented by what is called a 'codetta'.[1] Those repeated Amens which so often end a classical movement are a typical example. Our completed house looks like this:

Fig. 2

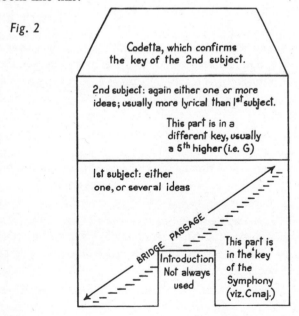

Codetta, which confirms the key of the 2nd subject.

2nd subject: again either one or more ideas; usually more lyrical than I\st subject.

This part is in a different key, usually a 5th higher (i.e. G)

1st subject: either one, or several ideas

BRIDGE PASSAGE

Introduction Not always used

This part is in the 'key' of the Symphony (viz. Cmaj.)

[1] A substantial example is called a 'coda', of which 'codetta' is merely a diminutive.

Once we have fully explored this set-up, our composer, like an over-eager host, says, 'I wonder, would you mind if we just went over it all again?' On the face of it, this would seem an unreasonable demand; why should we listen again to music we have only just heard? This is where we come to grips with the architectural aspect of music I have already mentioned. It is absolutely essential to our understanding of the symphony, sonata or quartet we are listening to that we should be able to store in our memories the exact proportions and relationships of the material the composer has presented to us. Keeping to the simile of the house, we must know where every bit of furniture is, the size of the rooms, the colour of the wall-papers, the pattern of the curtains; otherwise we shall never appreciate the significance of what is still to come. Of course nowadays we feel that we are so familiar with the classical repertoire that we tend to omit this custom of repeating the exposition, thereby doing neither our comprehension nor the work any great service. Only when we are truly sure of our knowledge of the first part of the movement should we venture into the exciting world which lies ahead.

The term Development, which is applied to the section we have now reached, should be self-explanatory; but since few people are capable of actually thinking in terms of music it remains somewhat vague in most listeners' minds. If I were to continue my simile of the house, I should say that development is akin to shifting the furniture around, redecorating the downstairs rooms, putting up new curtains, and adding a wing at the back. In other words, the composer takes the now familiar material of the exposition, and looks at it in a new light, pushing it around, changing its proportions, extending here, chopping there, until we have learnt a whole world of new truths about it. I feel that the most practical way I can show you what development really means is to take something that is familiar to you, and subject it to the sort of treatment it might receive from a classical composer. Here then is the immortal Daisy, still withholding her answer to the classic question.[1]

[1] Music quoted by kind permission of Francis, Day & Hunter Ltd.

Ex. 1

Dai - - sy,   Dai - - sy,   give me your an-swer do ____

Now the first four bars immediately suggest a sequence that would enable the composer to shift through various keys. (Again I should like to remind you that I shall be dealing with 'keys' and 'tonality' at the end of this chapter.) Without altering the original shape, one could do something on these lines:

Ex.2

Allegro con fuoco

(Dai-sy, Dai-sy)

(Daisy double speed)

etc.

Material like this, built on what is called the common chord—the notes a bugle plays—are the stock-in-trade of every classical composer. Daisy can be married to the tragic events of a Beethoven symphony without too much trouble.

Ex.3

Dai - - sy

Dai - - sy   etc.

A more serene treatment such as might appeal to Brahms would be found in this rather denser texture:

Now so far I have only suggested ways of treating the first limb of the tune; what about the second part, the 'Give me your answer, do' bit? Taking just this much of the phrase,

Ex. 5

it is a very simple matter to contrive something on these lines:

Or if you need something with more strength, what about this?

You will notice that both these last examples incorporate elements of the 'Daisy, Daisy' idea as well. This then is what is meant by the term Development, and it should be remembered that the examples I have given here are only a few of literally hundreds of possibilities that spring to a composer's mind when confronted with a combination of notes of this kind.

Returning to the subject of sonata form, from which this brief bicycle trip stemmed, we come now to the Recapitulation, which is perhaps the most misunderstood section of all. Many a thesis on the subject tends to imply that the Recapitulation is no more than a slavish reprise of the first few pages in which executants and audience alike can go to sleep without risk of missing anything of importance. Nothing could be further from the truth. Many a quickly made friendship has been reconsidered in the light of subsequent knowledge: the whole essence of sonata form as a drama is that the composer presents us with certain material in the Exposition; in the Development we get to know a great deal about it that we never dreamed of; in the Recapitulation we reassess the material *in the light of the experience gained*. I cannot overemphasize the importance of that statement. Once we have experienced the Development, once we have learnt the hidden secrets of the characters involved, once we have seen these relationships altered, we can never feel the same about them. In a play, we meet the characters in the first act; as it progresses, our feelings towards them change; new layers of character are revealed, showing heroism or weakness, treachery or loyalty. Now we know them as whole people, and by the time they take the curtain-call our conception of them can well have altered enormously. The same thing applies in music. A theme is like a living thing; one may find it difficult to feel affection for a tiny stunted clump of green in a flower-bed, but once it has grown into a great shrub covered with flowers one's feelings change to a glowing pride. The first two bars of Beethoven's Fifth Symphony are unremarkable enough; it is when we see what he makes of them that we salute a masterpiece.

One major structural alteration in the Recapitulation is perhaps worth mentioning at this stage, and that is the modification of the bridge passage. In order that he may avoid getting into a vicious circle of modulation, the composer has to make the second subject stay in the same 'key' as the first; consequently the staircase gets rebuilt, to turn back on itself.

Fig. 3

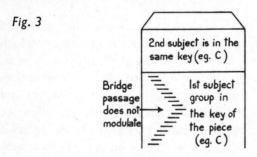

Few recapitulations are ever exact in proportions; most have several moments of surprise, often involving new 'development'.

We come now to this vital question of 'key' or 'tonality'. When we learn that a symphony is in D major or B flat minor it has more significance than a mere label, for to a composer 'key' is one of the most important elements in music—so much so that it takes on an almost mystical quality. Nobody can say exactly why keys possess the attributes they seem to have, but the most likely reason stems from the early days when music was written in keys with only one or two sharps or flats. Before the invention of what is known as 'Equal Temperament',[1] it was impossible to

---

[1] A method of tuning a keyboard so that it is imperceptibly out of tune, which makes the conflict between sharps and flats tolerable.

tune a keyboard instrument so that it could play in all keys and still be in tune; so the inaccessible keys acquired a quality of remoteness; they were lands into which a composer ventured at his peril. Ever since, the keys with a number of sharps and flats in their signature have possessed a slightly exotic quality; the simple keys are more 'everyday'. There is, however, more to it than that, and if you will bear with me a little longer we can investigate this mystery more fully. Again I should like to use the house as a simile, but this time there are twelve of them, built in a circle, like

Fig. 4

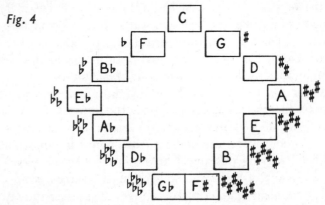

a newly planned housing estate. Each house has a resident, named as you will see in the illustration, and the houses to the right represent what are called the 'sharp' keys (♯), those on the left the 'flat' (♭). You will see that C has no sharps or flats; in other words, it is entirely on the white notes of the piano. G has one sharp which means that it has one note different from C; E has four sharps, which means that four of its notes are different from the scale of C. The same principle applies on the flat side. B flat has two flats, i.e. two notes in its scale are different from the scale of C. The bottom house is a semi-detached residence inhabited by two identical twins, G flat and F sharp. On the piano they are the same note, but written differently. It is easy to see why their scales are identical, since by now, in our journey 'away' from C, we find that these two keys have six notes different from C major, and as there are only seven notes in a scale, the mere fact of six being changed from the original departure-point will not allow for any alternatives.

In a classical sonata, or for that matter in most suites and many other forms of music, the first subject will be in a particular key and the next important theme, call it the second subject or what you will, will be in the house next-door in a clockwise direction. If a Bach allemande begins in B♭, half-way through it will arrive at F; if a Mozart sonata has the first subject in A, the second will be in E. This relationship is one of the great unwritten laws of music; the keys are closely related because, as you can see, there is only one note different in their two scales. The key you start in is called the 'Tonic', from the word Tone; the adjacent one is called the 'Dominant'. The house next-door in an *anti*-clockwise direction is called the Sub-dominant, and these three keys (e.g. C, F, and G, or A♭, E♭, and D♭) have such an interdependence on one another that the music can pass from the key of C to the key of G, or from C to F, almost without the listener being aware of it.

So far so good; where the housing estate comes into its own as a means of clarifying this aspect of music is when we come to analyse the effect of a distant modulation—a journey *across* the estate. The moment that a composer moves the music from say C major to G♭ major, he has stepped into a wildly remote land; in his terms it is a major talking-point—as though the village gossips were to say, 'What *was* Mr C doing visiting Miss D Flat's house at that time of night?' You can appreciate the impact of this by playing 'The Bluebells of Scotland' in the modified version below.

Ex.8

The ear at once tells you that something disastrous has happened; the earth has given way beneath your feet, and for the moment what you might call your 'tonal orientation' has been vastly disturbed.

You can understand then that this business of modulation, of moving into remote keys, is an important weapon in the composer's armoury; the most dramatic moment in a symphony or sonata is not necessarily the loudest; often it is a hushed chord emerging from a silence, but a chord in a key remote from the original starting-point.[1]

Two aspects of tonality remain, and then we can feel equipped to tackle a symphony intelligently. The first concerns what are known as 'minor' keys. Turn back to Fig. 4, and you will find that the relationship is easier to follow. If a piece is in C minor, it means that the resident of the house marked C is irresistibly drawn towards the house marked Eb; he becomes so obsessed with it that he begins to lose the essential qualities of 'C-ness'. A minor key always means that the house three doors away in an *anti-clockwise* direction casts a great shadow over the original. G minor is G clouded or obsessed by the essential elements of Bb; B minor is B influenced by D. Db minor is a difficult one. Count three along in an anti-clockwise direction, counting the Gb/F♯ house as one; you will arrive at E, which is a 'sharp' key. A composer will always think of Db minor as C♯ minor for this reason; Db and C♯ are only two names for the same note on the piano; Ex. 9 shows

Ex.9

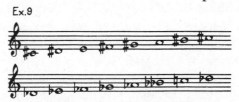

<hr/>

[1] Modulation can also give a quite tangible effect of 'journeying' in music; turn back to Ex. 2 and you will find that the apparent visual symmetry of the right-hand part is made not only tolerable but positively exciting by its movement from one 'key' to another. The first bar is in G major; in the next bar, the G♯ switches us towards A minor (bar 3). The G♯ in the bass in bar 2 strikes a responsive echo in bar 4 with the note Ab. This is the same note on the keyboard, and it is here used rather like a pun, a note with two meanings; as G♯ it took us to A minor; as Ab it takes us to F minor (bar 4) and then through Ab to Db major (bars 5-7). If you follow this journey round the 'housing estate' in Fig. 1, you will see that it takes us diametrically across. The progression is G→C (=A minor)→Ab (=F minor)→Db. The next paragraph explains 'minor' keys.

two versions of the scale of C♯ minor, one written in flats and one in sharps. You will see at once why the sharps are easier to read and to write.

One useful aspect of the minor keys is that they enable a composer to journey to remote keys more smoothly. For instance, if Mozart begins a tune in F major, and then changes it to F minor, which is a smooth and acceptable change, he has thereby shifted the music three steps towards the 'darker' keys of D♭ or G♭. He is that much farther away from home.[1]

The use of the word 'darker' brings me to the last point about tonality. We have already seen how the keys with a large number of sharps or flats came to have an exotic quality (see p. 19). The undeniable fact emerges that certain keys have emotional connotations in composers' minds; this is so profoundly a part of a musician's instinct that it even makes a difference when we come to the apparently similar keys of G♭ and F♯. Ask a concert pianist to try 'thinking' the last section of César Franck's Symphonic Variations in G flat major instead of F sharp, and he will think you are mad: it just wouldn't seem right. Yet the actual notes the hands play would be the same: only the thought behind them would alter. Fig 5 gives an indication of the sort of mood we can legitimately expect to associate with the cycle of keys.

Naturally there is no absolute hard-and-fast rule about this; also it must be realized that during the latter part of the nineteenth century these distinctions became less and less apparent; the whole key system was beginning to break down, and the so-called 'chromatic' music of Liszt and Wagner moved so rapidly from key to key that there was no longer any significance in modulation as such. The logical conclusion was the 'atonal' music of Schönberg and his disciples which jettisoned the key system entirely.

Now it would seem that I have spent an inordinate amount of time discussing first movement structure; surely the other movements deserve equal consideration? Curiously enough they do not;

---

[1] It is worth mentioning that E♭ major is called the 'relative major' of C minor. In a symphony in a minor key the second subject will usually be in the relative major rather than the dominant; a symphony in C major would have the second subject in G; a symphony in C minor would have the second subject in E♭.

Fig. 5

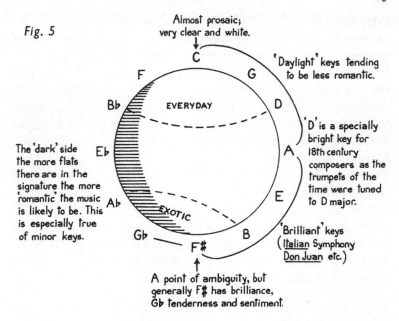

Almost prosaic;
very clear and white.

C

F   G

'Daylight' keys tending
to be less romantic.

Bb   EVERYDAY   D

'D' is a specially
bright key for
18th century
composers as the
trumpets of the
time were tuned
to D major.

Eb   A

The 'dark' side
the more flats
there are in the
signature the more
'romantic' the music
is likely to be. This
is especially true
of minor keys.

Ab

E

EXOTIC

Gb   B

F#

'Brilliant' keys
(Italian Symphony
Don Juan etc.)

A point of ambiguity, but
generally F# has brilliance,
Gb tenderness and sentiment.

in nearly every case it is the first movement which is the hard intellectual core of a symphony. The other movements have a more purely entertaining function. The way that Beethoven adapted the Minuet-and-Trio to his own purposes, thereby creating the new form of the Scherzo, is too well known to need any laborious description here; slow movements are normally easy to listen to, being more openly melodic than any other part of a symphony; the finale may be in sonata form, or it can be a rondo, or variations. Normally it is happy or triumphant in mood, since the composer is human enough to wish to excite his audience into an enthusiastic reception of his work.

To sum up, listening to a symphony means concentration; it means storing up in your memory each musical event in turn, for it is necessary to appreciate change and growth as they occur; form is significant, deviation from form even more so. Composers delight in laying traps for the unwary listener; often Beethoven or Mozart will present us with three similar phrases; just as you feel you can confidently predict what will happen next, they will whip the ground from beneath your feet by twisting the music in an unexpected direction. Also important, but so far unmentioned, is a sense of period. Harmonies that might pass unnoticed in a Schubert score may well be revolutionary in Mozart; we need to try and approach each work with an awareness of its pristine qualities—after all, everything was 'modern' once. There are some kinds of music, 'entertainment' music, which are not so demanding; but a symphony is the equivalent of a philosophical treatise, however seductive its sounds may be. I do not expect to read Ian Fleming and Bertrand Russell with an exactly similar approach; obviously one demands far greater concentration than the other. When you hear a symphony by a great composer you are listening to the thoughts of a major intellect speaking to you in a highly specialized language. Do not be so beguiled by the sound of his voice that you pay no heed to the words he is uttering; do not confuse the sound of music with its sense.

CHAPTER II

HAYDN

Symphony No. 86 in D (c. 1786)

1. Adagio leading to Allegro Spiritoso. 2. Capriccio (Largo).
3. Menuetto (Allegretto). 4. Finale (Allegro con spirito).

Orchestra: 1 flute; 2 oboes; 2 bassoons; 2 horns; 2 trumpets;
2 timpani: normal complement of strings.

This symphony is one of a set of six written for a concert-giving
organization in Paris, *Les Concerts de la Loge Olympique*. Robbins
Landon, the foremost authority on Haydn, classifies it as one of
the finest symphonies Haydn ever wrote.

I T WAS REALLY HAYDN who was most responsible for lifting
the status of the symphony from a glorified suite to a work of
real stature. Evidence of its derivation is still clear in the titles
which he attached to some of the movements in this work, but
no one can doubt from the very first page that this symphony is
a composition of real significance. Admittedly there are occasional patches of the rustic rum-tum-tum that is liable to crop up
when Haydn is in one of his less sophisticated moods; but they
are more than counterbalanced by some of his finest and most
imaginative passages, scattered freely throughout the score.

He begins with a solemn adagio to get the audience into a
suitably serious frame of mind;[1] but here is no conventional blare
of horn, trumpet, and kettledrum, but an introduction scored with
the utmost delicacy. At first glance it would appear to be a conventional opening, merely establishing the tonality of D major, as a
card-player might say which suit was trumps. But then as we look
closer at the score we find some very subtle touches; the tune is

---

[1] A perfect example of a 'front-door'; see p. 12.

on the first violins and two oboes. Marked at the unexpectedly low volume of *piano*, it is accompanied by plucked chords on the lower strings, alternating with quaver rests. It is one of the maxims of teaching composition that one should 'let the air in'; to have everyone playing all the time produces a porridge-like consistency, and Haydn here lightens the texture of the music, thereby allowing the tune to come through clearly without needing to be *forte*. Not until the eighth bar do we really sense the weight of the full orchestra, and the dignity and grandeur of this moment is enhanced by the transparency of what has gone before. First the violins then the lower strings have sweeping scales that cut across the sustained harmonies supporting them on wind and brass; these are no empty convention, but grand heraldic gestures, like great banners dipping in salute.

The introduction lasts some twenty-one bars of slow 3/4 time— a little over a minute; finally the music comes to rest on three clear chords of A major, the dominant of D. The stage has now been set for the first movement proper, and at this point Haydn could choose several alternatives; the most likely course would be to have a sudden strong allegro, clearly based on D major harmony— something like this perhaps:

Ex. 10

Another possibility would be a quiet bustle of excitement such as we find at the start of the overture to *The Marriage of Figaro*. The one thing we can be almost certain of is that the new theme will be unequivocally in the key of D major. However, Haydn, in common with many another great composer, depends upon us expecting this, and it delights him to foil our expectations by giving us something completely unforeseen instead. Having paved the way most carefully for a D major entrance, probably of some pomp and majesty when we remember those 'banners', he now gives us a handsome surprise in the shape of a quiet, frivolous theme whose harmony utterly contradicts D major, since its bass note is actually D sharp.

Ex. II

A comparison of Exx. 10 and 11 will clearly show the difference between orthodoxy and genius; the first is predictable and uninspired, the second shows the hand of a master.

To a knowledgeable listener, this will have been a considerable shock, and Haydn is now quick to show that all is forgiven and that he means no real harm; effortlessly he steps back into D major (see Ex. 11, bar 4), as though never for a moment had he contemplated doing anything else. The rest of the orchestra seem profoundly relieved to find order thus restored, and they all come bouncing in with a very rustic delight in a passage which shows little of the subtlety which preceded it. For twenty-seven bars they chug on merrily with a good deal of sound and fury signifying not very much. The section ends with a typical cadence rounding things off.

Ex. 12

At this point we have every justification for imagining that the second subject is about to appear; all the signs are there—we've reached the dominant key of A, we've had what sounded like a rather blustering bridge-passage, and this single repeated E and its attendant diminuendo suggest some new event. Again I will underline the wit of Haydn's music by suggesting a less inspired alternative.

Ex. 13

That is attractive enough, but again its compliance with the 'rules', however imaginary they may be, deprives it of spice. Haydn prefers something infinitely more unexpected; without a note of warning, he whips us back to the opening idea again, and just as before, it is once more in a contradictory key.

Ex. 14

By doing this, Haydn defers the arrival of the second subject so as to heighten its effectiveness when it ultimately arrives. When it does appear, it proves to be a graceful dance-like affair, with each phrase preceded by a little hopping up-beat.

Ex. 15

The graceful mood doesn't last long, however, and the codetta or tail-piece is very stormy before the main exposition ends.

Many Haydn works have a relatively short development section, but in this case there is an elaborate and dramatic development which concerns itself with most of the important material from the exposition. Initially, it concentrates on the 'surprise' idea

in Ex. 11, but just as the music is becoming positively spiritual
with a mysterious cadence in C sharp major,

Ex.16

the rustic rum–tum–tum theme comes bounding back again. This
effectively rules the roost until Haydn comes to a charming
example of the sort of double bluff one often finds in classical
music. You will remember how he avoided the predictable in
Ex. 14; how just as you were expecting the second subject he shot
back to the opening theme? What then would you anticipate at
this apparently similar moment?

Ex.17

With complete confidence you could assert that at this point
you are prepared to hear the first theme again, exactly as you do
in bars 3 and 4 of Ex. 14. Haydn knows this as well as you do, so
with enchanting waywardness he once again foils expectation and
does what he *ought* to have done originally—he leads into the
second subject.

Ex.18

One can almost hear him say, 'Fooled again!' It is points like
these that so perfectly illustrate the importance of memory and
comparison in listening to a work of this nature. More than half
the joy of listening to this symphony lies in an appreciation of
Haydn's dexterity in avoiding the obvious. Despite the seemingly
conventional idiom of the music, so easily dismissed as the routine
formality of eighteenth-century composition, every page is full of
subtle and highly personal touches; but they need a cultivated ear

to spot them, and since they are nearly always concerned with comparing this phrase with that, they need also the ability to review the whole movement as one span.

This is less likely to be true of the later movements. Nearly always the first movement of a symphony contains the toughest fibre; it is not too fanciful to suggest that at this period the symphony was expected to represent the whole of man. The first movement is his intellect, the second his sensuality, the third his manners, and the finale his sense of fun. Thus one finds development of small thematic units in the opening movement, the sensuous beauty of extended melody in the second, the formal grace of the minuet in the third, and a gay or even boisterous rondo to round off the picture. It is for this reason that analytical essays such as these tend to spend far longer on first movements than on any others—they are so much more complex.

In this symphony the second movement is marked Largo and Capriccio, two apparently contradictory terms, since to be capricious very slowly would savour of a paradox. In fact, nothing very capricious happens; the term is merely Haydn's justification for the overt emotionalism of the movement. Such is its freedom of key and melody, such its tenderness and passion, that he must have felt that sensuousness of this order might seem out of place in a serious work. Right from the start he has one of those heart-turning phrases which have a profoundly emotional effect by dint of their very simplicity. To an ear dulled by a surfeit of Tchaikovsky and Chopin, these harmonies may seem nothing special; once again it takes a subtle response to modulation and dissonance to fully appreciate Haydn's skill. He begins in un-ashamed G major:

Ex.19

but then in the second bar, he suddenly passes a shadow over the phrase, only to release the tension a moment later.

Ex.20

The asterisk marks the tension-point, the twist of the knife in the wound; without this it would be colourless; with it, it is infinitely touching. Again the scoring is miraculous, allowing the sustained lines to stand out clearly against the detached chords beneath.

Soon the mood changes to that of a formal dance, replete with the elaborate gestures of the period, simple in outline but complex in detail. However, do not be deceived by the apparent effortlessness of all this. There are big happenings ahead, and some very startling surprises to catch the indolent listener napping. Here is an example; at this point Haydn seems to be heading for a nice sit-down in D major, but as you see he averts this by a sudden and unexpected chord of B flat.

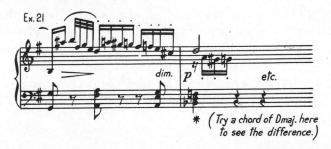

This is after all a fairly stock interrupted cadence, and we can survive worse shocks than that. It is enough though just to disturb our equilibrium, and now, while we are still off balance, Haydn really rocks us with an alarming shift of tonality and mood. The atmosphere becomes electric with drama, just as the calm of a summer evening can suddenly be dispelled by thunder.

Ex. 22

The prettiness and elegance of the preceding passages are only skin-deep; here is the stuff of tragedy and high drama. Like a clap of thunder, though, it is soon over; passages like this justify the name Capriccio for this movement. There are several such outbursts, but for the most part it is gentle and tender; some passages are as romantic as it is possible for a composer of this period to be. Look out for one section where the singing bass line of violas and 'cellos is accompanied by delicate little clashes in the violins above and sighs of passion from the oboe. Once again, though, there is a very ungentle outburst immediately afterwards, as if to show that mere sentiment is not enough. Perhaps these storms are only lovers' quarrels and not to be taken too seriously; the main thing to realize is that this movement shows Haydn at his most inspired; small wonder that it was received with enthusiasm by the Paris audiences of the time.

More unexpected are the treasures to be found in the next movement. The Menuet and Trio are so frequently a little four-square for present-day taste; it almost seems as though the confinement of a strict dance-form might have restricted the composers' imagination. In this instance, Haydn starts out formally enough with a dance rhythm calculated to set even the Duke of York's foot tapping—to whom, by the way, the work has sometimes (erroneously) alleged to have been dedicated. Nothing could be clearer than the initial rhythmic patterns of this movement; the experienced listener, familiar with Haydn's guile, will expect a trap. Sure enough, he has some more surprises for us. Just a little way into the second main stanza the rhythm suddenly seems to hesitate as though the players had lost all confidence.

Ex. 23

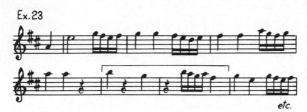

This subtle interruption of the symmetrical patterns just makes all the difference; no sooner has he broken the chain than he embarks on a shatteringly beautiful sequence in which he piles one delicate clash upon another; surely these are the pains of love of which the poets of the time made so much.

Ex. 24

Few composers have such a blend of sophistication and innocence in their music as Haydn; after the delicate subtlety of Ex. 24, the trio seems like music for peasants. It is straight dance-music, not all that different from what one might hear today in the Tyrol played on the accordion by a self-taught musician. Haydn never lost touch with the simple flavour of folk-music, and to find exquisitely wrought counterpoint side by side with rustic dances is quite the normal thing in his compositions. It is a sad commentary on the self-consciousness of contemporary music that such simplicity is no longer acceptable.

The last movement is like a children's game, gay and full of sparkling mischief. Again one cannot fail to be impressed by the delicacy of touch; Haydn deploys his comparatively slender resources with immense skill and economy. Remember that the horns and trumpets of the time were very limited in range and facility, so his occasional insistence on repeated notes is understandable. As always with such a composer one is constantly aware of the way in which a straightforward idea is given distinction. Here is a sequence which is merely a long ascending scale of two octaves; but how cleverly its simple bone-structure is disguised.

Ex. 25

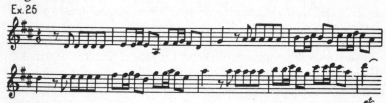

The second subject looks forward to the frivolity of Rossini; both Haydn and Mozart frequently use material which would readily transplant into an operatic score. Above all, the sheer high spirits of this movement leave the most lasting impression. It is all very well to call him Papa Haydn, but there was certainly a lot of the child still in him when he wrote music like this; it's young and fresh and tireless. Unlike some of the self-searching works of the nineteenth century, this was written for your enjoyment and delight. There is no room for sorrow, anguish, and introspection here; even the stormy moments in the Largo soon resolve into sunshine. Small wonder that he lived to a nice healthy old age when he had a spirit as eternally youthful as is revealed in this delectable score.

CHAPTER III

MOZART

Symphony in D (K.504), The 'Prague' (1786)

1. Adagio, leading to Allegro. 2. Andante. 3. Finale: Presto.

Orchestra: 2 flutes; 2 oboes; 2 bassoons; 2 horns; 2 trumpets; 2 timpani; normal complement of strings.

Completed on 6 December 1786 and presumably intended for a first performance in Prague on the occasion of his subsequent visit there in January of the following year. Both this and the preceding Haydn symphony bear testimony to the remarkable interchange of music between capital cities at a time when travelling was a matter of great discomfort; thus we find Haydn writing for Paris, Mozart for Prague.

S O MAGNIFICENT is the final great trilogy of symphonies[1] that Mozart wrote in six unbelievable weeks in 1788 that we tend to forget quite how perfect some of the earlier symphonies are. In the so-called 'Prague' symphony we find a splendid example of Mozart's mature orchestral writing; composed only five years before his death, it shows him as a master of every emotion and a matchless craftsman. It is neither as tragic as the fortieth symphony in G minor, nor as staggering in its intellectual mastery as the 'Jupiter'; it occupies a happy position between the two in which grace and beauty are married to a faultless technique.

Prague seems to have been a singularly fortunate city for Mozart; works which the fickle Viennese had failed to appreciate were received with rapture when transferred to the rival capital, and the huge success of The Marriage of Figaro in Prague must have encouraged Mozart, in sheer gratitude, to give particular attention

---

[1] The symphonies No. 39 in E♭, No. 40 in G minor, and No. 41 in C (the 'Jupiter').

to a symphony destined to have its first performance there.[1] Before making any attempt to analyse this symphony it would be a worth while step to discuss the art of listening as it affects this composer, whose music gives me personally the greatest pleasure of all.

Listening to Mozart is rather like walking along a hedgerow that is absolutely ablaze with wild flowers; you get several impressions, of which the most superficial is that this is just a hedge and as such hardly merits your notice. In this category come the people who regard Mozart as a light appetizer before getting down to a main meal of Beethoven, Brahms, and Tchaikovsky. Next you have the person who realizes that there are a lot of flowers about, but of a rather common kind; he is the one who dismisses Mozart as 'pretty', and regards the delicate eighteenth-century conventions of rococo decoration as merely trivial. Lastly you have the enthusiast who takes the trouble to examine each flower, observing the miraculous detail, savouring every aspect of its simple perfection.

In fact, there was never a composer so subtle in harmony, so elegant in thought as Mozart, and if we are to appreciate every nuance that is to be found in his scores, then we have got to be infinitely more responsive to detail than we are when we listen to a nineteenth-century work; for while the emotional content may be every bit as deeply felt as it is in Tchaikovsky's music, it will be expressed with far greater reticence. If I may digress for a moment into the pages of the 'Jupiter' symphony it will be possible to demonstrate the relationship between harmony and emotion fairly clearly. The third and fourth bars of the 'Jupiter' read as follows:

Ex.26

To an ear jaded by late nineteenth-century harmony these chords may seem ordinary enough, but in Mozart's time these

[1] On 17 January 1787.

sweet dissonances unquestionably had a highly emotional flavour. Play them slowly, and linger on the first and third beats of the bar; savour the interval of a seventh between D and C in the first chord, the even sharper clash in the second full harmony when the melody-note of D is sounded against the C and E beneath—in effect, three adjacent notes sounding simultaneously. The important thing to realize about these harmonies is that composers of a later age had to resort to more extreme chords to achieve the same emotional result. A classic example of the more expressive type of Romantic harmony is to be found in the opening bars of Wagner's *Tristan*.

Ex. 27

Different though they may be, the function of the chords in this and the preceding example is the same. In both cases the harmonies are points of emotional tension which is then relaxed, like hands clasped in the traditional (and universal) expression of grief.

Play these two examples at the same slow tempo and it is not difficult to see a similarity of effect; if Wagner's harmonic palette is richer, more 'advanced' than Mozart's, it is simply because the whole history of music shows a gradual extension of harmonic resources, a process of adding notes to previously existing chords, of thickening textures, even of extending the compass of the instruments themselves. Such a process was artistically essential since each composer of significance has the capacity to 'patent', as it were, certain sounds. When Beethoven began his fourth piano concerto with the chord of G major spaced in this particular way,

Ex. 28

he created a sound which could never be used again without instantly suggesting the opening of this concerto. It is an exclusive 'Beethoven' model, not to be copied. Anyone coming after him had to find a new way of spacing out that harmony, a way which would establish it as being in turn 'his'. Thus we find Stravinsky taking exactly the same components that Beethoven used, i.e. the notes G, B, and D, but reassembling them to produce a totally different sonority.

Ex.29
Slow

Now it so happened that Mozart arrived at a period in history when the type of harmony which we are accustomed to hearing in the great bulk of the normal concert repertoire was comparatively new and virginal. Just as the twentieth-century composer uses a different harmonic idiom from that of the nineteenth, so did Mozart use a type of harmony, and in particular a *texture* that had first begun to be formulated by Bach's sons. Listen to the music of J. C. Bach[1] and you can hear where Mozart learnt his style, a style which broke away completely from that established by the great John Sebastian. However, apart from Haydn, nobody of sufficient stature had yet appeared to develop these new resources of harmony and texture in anything like the same way that Mozart was able to; consequently he could achieve the maximum effect with the minimum effort.

It is vital that we should realize this, that we should reacquire the 'taste' of a Mozart harmony; for while the underlying emotion in his music is frequently 'romantic' in the deepest sense of the

[1] John Christian Bach (1735–82). J. S. Bach's youngest son; spent some time in London and greatly influenced the young Mozart when the Mozart family came to London in 1764.

word, he invariably expresses himself with infinitely greater economy and restraint than the post-Beethoven composer. In the first four bars of the 'Jupiter' symphony, Mozart expresses an alternation of heroism and tenderness; the heroism is not more heroic, nor the tenderness more tender if they happen in later years to be expressed in phrases twice as long on an orchestra double the size. All that happens is that the expression of the emotions concerned becomes that much more obvious. Mozart's music may display a world in miniature, but it is not a miniature world.

With these considerations in mind, our understanding of the 'Prague' symphony is likely to be enhanced; like the Haydn symphony discussed in the previous chapter (which was in all likelihood written in the same year), this work begins with a slow introduction. The tempo is the sole thing they have in common, however, for Haydn goes from lyricism to grandeur where Mozart goes from an imposing start to a tune of extreme pathos. Notice how in nearly every classical symphony the composer is at pains to establish a completely sure sense of tonality in the listener right from the start. Over and over again we find first themes or introductions based on a 'common chord' motif or repeated assertions of the tonic or keynote. Here Mozart reiterates the note D no fewer than five times, underlining it with an imposing triplet figure which almost suggests military pomp and splendour.

Ex.30

Most unexpectedly, the response to this arresting but immensely confident opening is a sequence of highly emotional chords, grouped in pairs like falling sighs, and leading in their turn to a haunting phrase on the first violins, accompanied by sympathetic chords on the lower strings. Nowhere else in the thirty-six bars of

this profound introduction does the confident feeling of the opening reappear; the mood remains intensely emotional, racked with
spasms of deep anguish in related minor keys, and with striking
alternations between ominous brass and pleading strings. When
one considers that trumpets and drums alike are confined to a
choice of two notes (D and A) throughout the stormy second half
of this introduction, one can only be amazed at the simplicity with
which Mozart achieves his effects.

Once we reach the allegro, thereby entering the first movement
proper, we find Mozart in a characteristically restless mood. The
violins fidget at the keynote, in uneasy syncopations that are only
slightly relieved when they ultimately flower into a little wisp of
melody.

(As a touching variation of this try playing A♯ for A♮ in bars
2-4 in the left hand, a subtle harmonic twist Mozart introduces
later.)

This same figure (Ex. 31, bars 5-6) is soon extended, while
above it Mozart introduces new material; he frequently uses links
of this nature, looking back over his shoulder at something that
has gone before and using it as a counter-melody to some new
idea. Regarding bars 5-6 of the preceding example as stage one, we
can trace this rhythmic pattern through stage two:

Ex.32

until in stage three, some pages later, we find traces of both these ideas, now further illuminated by a wonderfully lyrical counterpoint in the second violins. Notice here how the sustained line will glow through the texture of the music, simply by virtue of being surrounded with staccato phrases.

Ex.33

Not only is the serene beauty of the second violin line a marvellous foil to the more agile parts surrounding it, it also manages to give an extraordinary poignancy to what otherwise might seem a rather busy little passage, for with the utmost skill Mozart arranges a dissonance (and consequently an emotional tension) on each first beat. Isolate the chords marked with an asterisk and you will see what I mean.

Another enchanting example of this 'brought forward' technique appears when we come to the second subject. At a first glance this would seem to be a rather trivial tune.

Such simplicity is misleading, for Mozart merely regards the

Ex.34

melody so far as a starting-point. The first modification we find is when he puts it into the minor,[1] underlining its longer notes with sad little echoes on the bassoons; the magical surprise comes at the restoration of the major key which quickly ensues, for now, while bassoons take over the original melody, the violins produce an enchanting new counter-theme, so beguiling in shape that it could well be regarded as the true second subject.

In the development section of this symphony, Mozart amuses himself by adding a new element in which various pairs of instruments play prettily with daisy-chains of scales, continually overlapping and unwinding.

He then proceeds to work this against much of the material that we have had so far, more particularly the bustling little theme in bars 5-6 of Ex. 31. It is easy for a reasonably equipped theoretician to be a trifle condescending about a passage like the preceding example; after all, it represents a fairly orthodox trick of counterpoint. What is an especial delight in Mozart's music, though, is to see the way he transmutes these textbook tags into pure poetry. Many a worthy but uninspired organist would be capable of producing the type of imitation that is quoted above; only a genius of Mozart's calibre could take this same material and

[1] Thereby producing a close resemblance to the finale of Beethoven's Pianoforte Sonata, Op. 31, No. 2

change its very essence to something as full of pathos as this·

Ex.37

In the face of·harmonies like these, anyone who cannot bring himself to admit the essential Romanticism of Mozart's music is being wilfully blind. This study has not set out to be a bar-by-bar analysis of the first movement; the person who requires that might just as well buy a score and do it for himself. What I hope it has done is to pinpoint some of the reasons that cause me to be so enthusiastic about this and many other symphonies by Mozart. Counting the introduction, the movement is 302 bars long, or thirty-one pages of miniature score. Within this comparatively short span are contained passages as stormy as Beethoven, as lyrical as Schubert, as gay as Rossini, as emotional as Liszt or Wagner; all these are expressed in an idiom so elegant in style, so utterly distinguished in thought, so without ostentation or emotional self-indulgence that the mind of the understanding listener will never tire of the infinite variety concealed beneath its delectable surface.

Somewhat unusually for a symphony of this period, the 'Prague' has only three movements, a scheme which might be due to some special planning on Mozart's part, but which more probably was occasioned by the rapid approach of his visit to Prague, and his consequent eagerness to finish the symphony at all costs, even if he had to dispense with the conventional Menuet and Trio. Certainly there is no evidence of hurry in the slow movement itself; it is unusually rich in decoration and harmony, recalling the mood of some of the more contemplative arias in the operas. As always, his deployment of the orchestra is astonishingly colourful when one considers how relatively new the art of orchestration was. This may seem a rather provocative statement, but a dispassionate consideration of Bach's use of the orchestra in the Brandenburg Concertos or the Suites makes one realize that he could be quite indiscriminate in the way he transferred music from one instrument to another. Oboe parts and string parts were completely interchangeable; and the grand old man of Leipzig was quite happy to have his entire band playing complex counterpoint for half a dozen pages on end. The result is sometimes a somewhat indigestible porridge of semiquavers which intertwine with a relentlessness that defies even the most well-intentioned performers. Look at bars 30–61 of the first Brandenburg Concerto and you will see an example of the sort of passage I mean. This is not to say that Bach was not capable of imaginative colouring when he put his mind to it; nevertheless, orchestration was not a primary consideration for him.

Mozart's use of soft holding-notes on horns or wind produces a lovely blend of sound, and his melodic line is constantly changing in colour, from violins to flute, flute to oboe, then to bassoon or 'cellos. On occasion he will use the strings in unison against sustained harmony in the wind and brass; but whereas earlier composers would most probably have conceived such a combination as being suitable for loud passages only, Mozart uses it for quiet mystery and a complete change of texture. Admittedly Haydn too was extraordinarily inventive in his orchestration at times, but he had the benefit of a permanent orchestra to experiment with; much that Haydn must have learned from experience Mozart seems to have divined by instinct.

The slow movement of the 'Prague', an Andante in 6/8 time, starts with an interesting example of a subtle balance between what are called diatonic and chromatic notes. (Diatonic notes are those which 'belong' to a particular scale, chromatic notes are outsiders, and have the exotic quality which one always attributes to foreigners. In the scale of C, the white notes on the keyboard are the diatonic, the black notes are chromatic. The diatonic notes are associated with simplicity and the direct statement; the chromatic with more highly coloured matters, whether they be pathetic or stormy.) Mozart begins this movement with an extremely simple-looking pastoral phrase, which, for its first two bars, preserves an unsullied aspect of G major; he then introduces a welter of chromatic notes, thereby adding an element of decorative sophistication which brings the music back from the country into the concert-hall. The deceptive simplicity of much of this music should not hoodwink us into believing that Mozart was simple; there is not a bar in which his conscious, if effortless, technique is not apparent. The placing of each modulation, the balance between stillness and movement, the calculated increase of emotion brought about by decoration, the uncanny selection of harmonies that just evade the obvious—all these are the hall-marks of a superlative craftsman. A detailed analysis would be boring; get hold of a score, and study it with a resolute determination to take nothing for granted.

The finale shows Mozart in an unusual mood, nearer to Beethoven's boisterousness than his fastidious taste normally allowed him to go. It begins with the type of eager bustle that we find so often in the operas.

Ex.38

This phrase, with its innocent eagerness, he soon tries to blast
off the face of the earth with a series of gigantic blows. Savage
though these sound, I cannot believe they are really meant to be
taken seriously. It is the ferocious roar of a child wearing a mask,
quite different from the alternations of *ff* and *p* that we find in
Beethoven's Fifth Symphony. Only at one point does Mozart
seem to become caught up in a real paroxysm of anger, and at
that moment we find something uncannily near to Beethoven at
his most awe-inspiring. The difference between the simulation of
anger and the real thing is quite easy to spot. When we hear one
sustained chord at a time in brass and wind lasting for four bars,
then we are witnessing sheer braggadocio; when on the other
hand we find that same chord repeated, worried at like this,

I think we can safely assume that the frivolity of much of the movement has been for the moment put aside. Alfred Einstein goes so
far as to say that this movement, despite all its appearance of
cheerfulness, leaves 'a wound in the soul'; in it, 'beauty is wedded
to death'.[1] At the risk of seeming to contradict one of the world's
great authorities on Mozart, I would suggest that that is an over-
statement as far as this particular movement is concerned. There
are many works of Mozart in which I feel that the phrase 'tears
behind the smile' describes the emotion conveyed by the music.
In this symphony, however, I feel that he went deep enough in
the first movement; surely the finale is a joyful offering to the
people of Prague, a people who welcomed him in their midst and
who loved him and his music. With his thoughts winging towards
them and the excitement of a production of *Don Giovanni* ahead

[1] Alfred Einstein: *Mozart: his character and work*: Cassell, 1946.

of him, I have the impression that this finale at least can be taken too seriously. In its one passage of genuine terror the music would seem to have got a little out of hand; but all is quickly forgiven and one carries away the memory of a sunlit work, full of a radiance that is hard to equal.

CHAPTER IV

BEETHOVEN

Symphony No. 3 in E♭ (Op. 55), The 'Eroica'

1. Allegro con brio. 2. Marcia funebre; Adagio assai. 3. Scherzo and Trio; Allegro vivace. 4. Finale; Allegro molto—Poco andante, con espressione—Presto (Variations).

Orchestra: 2 flutes; 2 oboes; 2 clarinets; 2 bassoons, 3 horns; 2 trumpets; 2 timpani; normal complement of strings—by now more than either Haydn or Mozart would have had.

Started in the summer of 1803, finished by the spring of the following year; second only to his Ninth Symphony in dimensions and substantially bigger in scope than anything written before it. This was probably the first time three horns had been used in the orchestra; note also the now standard acceptance of clarinets—instruments that were only invented in Mozart's time, and consequently only used by him in five of his forty-one symphonies.

So MUCH HAS ALREADY been written about Beethoven and his music that it seems almost presumptuous to add anything else to the pile; the fact remains, however, that there are always new listeners to be catered for, not to mention the many thousands of music-lovers who, while they may be familiar with the sound of the Beethoven symphonies, have still never read any of the books by Grove, Tovey, Dickinson, Riezler, Schauffler, Evans, and the many other writers who together have contributed the 200 treatises, analyses, biographies, character studies, and essays that are listed in Grove's Dictionary alone. If, then, some of the material in this essay is already known to you, have consideration for those for whom even the background of this famous symphony may still be only vaguely realized.

It is difficult when we think about Beethoven's music not to be influenced by the extraordinary facts of his life. If a Hollywood film producer had invented a story in which a man who was to be generally regarded as the world's greatest composer was made stone deaf for half his creative life, not only the critics but also the general public would have thought it pretty far-fetched. A dumb poet would be a little more probable, a blind artist a little less. A deaf composer is a mockery of the gods—an object of pity if his talent is small, but a tragedy on a Grecian scale when he is one of the greatest creators of all time. Yet this deafness undoubtedly gives us a clue to many of the more baffling problems that his music presents; can we be surprised that the terrible birth-pangs which his compositions had to survive made his music unlike anyone else's?

Despite the hopelessness of his situation, Beethoven never gave up trying to have a physical contact with music. Even though he could no longer hear a note, he used to supervise rehearsals of his works, watching like a hawk, relating the movements of the players to the imagined sounds in his head. A violinist called Böhm, the leader of a quartet who used to play Beethoven's later compositions (in spite of considerable hostility from the public), tells us of a rehearsal of the Eb quartet, Op. 127. The work had been played once at a concert but was regarded as a meaningless fiasco, so the players went to Beethoven for coaching. Böhm had an idea that Beethoven's directions at the end of the work were wrong. The composer had put *Meno vivace*—less quickly—and Böhm felt that this slowing up of the music weakened its effect. He told the other members of the quartet to stick to the same tempo, and see what Beethoven said. Imagine the barely furnished room, cluttered with heaps of music and manuscript paper; in the middle, the four musicians playing, and in a corner the squat broad figure of the composer. His face is scarred with smallpox, his clothes are shabby beyond belief, his hair unkempt; but the eyes, deepset beneath bushy eyebrows, are staring at the performers with intense concentration. Every movement of their hands and fingers is related in his mind to the music he has written but never heard. In Böhm's own words: 'Beethoven, crouched in a corner, heard nothing, but watched with strained attention. After the last stroke of the bows, he said laconically, "Let it remain so", went to the desks and crossed out the *Meno vivace* in the four parts.'

This story, which is undoubtedly authentic, gives us some idea of the sort of concentration Beethoven must have had. Think of watching a film without a sound-track, a film of a string-quartet, and having to work out from the movements of the players exactly what and how they are playing, and you will get an impression of what he must have endured. What torture it must have been for this man to watch this dream-like performance of music he had never heard, nor ever would hear. It was not until 1822 that the final impact of total deafness struck him brutally at a rehearsal of *Fidelio* which he was bravely attempting to conduct. It was impossible to work under him, and finally his friend Schindler handed him a note, saying, 'I beg you not to go on; will explain at home.' Like a knife, the message cut through Beethoven's dreams and he rushed from the theatre, to collapse in tears of bitterest anguish at his house. In his later works the bearing of such a monstrous burden seemed to give him a super-natural strength, an ability to explore the profoundest depths of human suffering, yet still to attain a divine peace.

At the time of the 'Eroica' Symphony, the picture was not quite so black. His deafness had begun, but was still not total; he had won through the first spiritual struggle which the onset of his disease had brought in its train. The first agony of mind, which is so heartbreakingly conveyed in the famous *Heiligenstadt Testament* of October 1802, had been overcome. He was reconciled to his fate, and the sunlit gaiety of the Second Symphony, written when he was in the depths of despair, had proved to be a remedy more potent than anything medical science had to offer. With extra-ordinary resolution he planned, as he put it, to start upon 'a new road'; he remembered a commission given some four years previously, when the French ambassador in Vienna, General Bernadotte, had suggested that he might compose a symphony in honour of Napoleon. At the time Beethoven looked on the French leader as a saviour of his people; all his revolutionary instincts spoke in sympathy with the struggle the French had had to shake off the aristocratic tyranny they had endured too long. By the spring of 1804 the new symphony was finished, and one day Beethoven's disciple Ries saw a fair copy of the score lying on the master's piano. The title-page simply contained two names: at the top, 'Buonaparte'; at the bottom, 'Luigi[1] van Beethoven'. Here then was the tribute from one great man to another, a tribute unadorned by flowery speeches that might smack of insincerity. Only a few days later the idol proved to have feet of clay; on 18 May of that year Napoleon assumed the title of Emperor; when Beethoven heard the news he flew into a rage. 'After all, then,' he cried, 'he is nothing but an ordinary mortal! He will trample the rights of man underfoot, and become a greater tyrant than anyone.' Stamping across the room, he seized the score and tore the title-page in half. This tattered relic still exists and bears silent witness to the truth of the story. In the end, the work appeared as a 'Heroic symphony, composed to preserve the memory of a great man,[2] and dedicated to his Serene Highness Prince Lobkowitz'—one of Beethoven's patrons. It is one of the ironies of fate that the symphony that was designed to celebrate the end of much that the aristocracy stood for should ultimately be dedicated to a prince, even if he was a beneficent patron of the arts.

The first movement begins with two great chords of E♭ major. Beethoven's first sketches for the symphony show an interesting variation; his original idea was that these two chords should be based on dominant harmony; what is more, they were unevenly spaced.

Ex.40

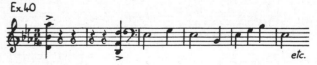

etc.

[1] A curious eccentricity on Beethoven's part since he normally signed himself Ludwig.
[2] *Composta per festeggiare il Sovvenire di un grand'Uomo.*

Apparently he then became worried by the gap between the first and second chords, and experimented with the possibility of filling it with some vaguely suggested notes.

Ex.41

Fortunately this unconvincing alternative was scrapped, and the infinitely stronger opening that we now know was finally devised. The brief introduction over, we hear the principal theme of the movement on the 'cellos. Like most classical symphonic material it is based on a common chord. Mozart at the age of twelve had hit on a remarkably similar theme at the start of his little opera *Bastien and Bastienne*. To compare them is an apt demonstration of the difference between charm and strength. Mozart, thirty-five years earlier, had written this:

Ex.42

All is tranquil and serene; the even measures of dance music suggest elegant behaviour in aristocratic circles. Compare the Beethoven to that, and what a storm is there, with the sudden twist to the foreign note of C♯, and the agitation of the syncopated G's in the violins above.

Ex.43

Here, then, are two conflicting ideas; the assurance of E♭ major once established is then undermined by the dissenting C♯; at once the violins reflect the uneasiness which this unexpected note inevitably brings. The almost pastoral mood of the opening is deceptive; it is as though the sculptor were caressing the stone with his hands before striking the first hammer-blows which will hew it into shape. By the twenty-fifth bar we find strongly accented chords breaking across the beat—

until finally the first theme returns in triumph.

It is already idle to speculate on any episode in Napoleon's career which these violent changes of mood might represent. The stimulus to Beethoven's imagination was no more than a 'trigger' action; once the musical material entered his head he would have been unlikely to have had thoughts for any external sequence of events. Commentators of the time produced fantastic theories about the work, such as the seriously made suggestion that Napoleon's army had arrived in Egypt by the time the Development had been reached since one of its episodes was a theme of 'decidedly Oriental colouring'. If the violent cross-accentuation of the preceding example indicates a battle it is indeed a brief one, since in a matter of twenty bars the mood relents and we discover a charming section in which each of the woodwind in turn plays a little three-note phrase, like children passing a toy from hand to hand to be admired.

This of course is a quickened-up version of bars 4-5 of Ex. 43. But we must not pay too much attention to detailed phrases in this score, fascinating though their relationships may be. It is a huge canvas on a generous scale, and one of its most remarkable features is the way in which Beethoven changes its mood with the utmost frequency and yet welds the whole vast movement together completely satisfactorily. In the next hundred bars or so we find a great variety of new ideas. In addition to the three-note phrase above, there is this rising scale on clarinets,

which is mirrored in descending bassoons; this is followed by a far more athletic phrase for the strings,

and by way of further contrast a positively Mendelssohnian little theme

which might be labelled the 'true' second subject were it not for the fact that Beethoven never uses it again till the Recapitulation. Varied though these fragments may seem detached from their context in this way, the fact remains that in the course of the movement they appear to follow on one after the other in a marvellously natural and spontaneous way. Remember, though, that nothing like this had ever been done before under the title of Symphony, and it is particularly suitable that this revolution in symphonic form should have been written to celebrate the most famous son of a revolution.

The Development begins mysteriously with ghostly echoes of the rhythm of the opening theme; however, far and away the most useful idea is the athletic rhythm of Ex. 47. This Beethoven uses as a unifying force; up to now, he hasn't revealed to us that it will fit against the 'cellos' opening phrase. The more excitable rhythm has an inflammatory effect, and the pastoral mood of the first few notes is transformed into a veritable tempest.

Ex.49

Intermittently the sheer volume of sound created here is reduced to a sudden *piano*, but at such moments the music is still too disturbed to subside entirely and little flickers of restlessness persist in the second violins. One of the most remarkable passages in the movement comes a little later on; its revolutionary aspect is enhanced by a nice piece of symbolism. Beethoven starts what appears to be a fugue, albeit an agitated and fiery one.

Ex.50

Within thirteen bars of its inception this ordered counterpoint is engulfed in a storm of passion. It is as though all shackles with the past were being violently broken; 'modern' chords shatter the ancient traditions of fugue. Like a Samson shaking the very foundations of harmony, Beethoven wrestles with the music in a passage such as had never been heard before. Dissonances of extraordinary violence pound across the natural feel of the rhythm, and for more than thirty bars the framework of the music seems to be battered out of shape. Finally, all passion spent, a forlorn little tune emerges in the remote key of E minor, a tune which in my opinion seldom seems to be interpreted with quite the feeling of exhaustion which its position implies.

Ex.51

This is the innocent wisp of melody which suggested the Ancient Nile to a mid-nineteenth-century critic!

The other really outstanding moment in this wonderful movement comes just before the return home to the Recapitulation. For some time we have had the impression that something is in the air; the music seems almost overcome by a feeling of inertia, and then, tentative and distant, the horns breathe the first four notes of the opening theme. This is the famous 'wrong-note' entry that caused so much comment when it was first heard. The actual notes are these:

Ex. 52

It is pathetic to see how petty minds have tried to 'correct' Beethoven's wonderfully picturesque touch. At the level of a first-year harmony student, one could say that the chord above the horn entry doesn't 'fit'; but why a man of Wagner's stature should have suggested that Beethoven had really intended the second violins to have G instead of A♭ in those two vital bars is beyond me. Other nineteenth-century authorities thought the horn part was intended to be in the tenor clef, which would make it read B♭DB♭F. Both emendations seem incredibly narrow-

minded. Even the devoted disciple Ries suggested at the first
rehearsal of the work that 'the damned horn-player' had come in
wrong. Beethoven's only reply was to aim a terrific clout at him,
which fortunately missed. Once it is divorced from considerations
of textbook harmony, what a wonderful effect this moment is;
the gradual reduction of the orchestral texture to a whisper, then
faint and evocative the distant horn-call which is instantly received
with a great shout of acclamation by the rest of the orchestra.
Here, one might say, is a moment that does savour of 'programme'
music, as though a great concourse of people awaited the arrival
of their hero, and at the distant sound of his fanfare, shouted aloud.

In triumph the original theme returns, but with a marvellously
subtle change which seems to symbolize an easing of its inner
conflict. The C♯ in bars 5-6 of Ex. 43 no longer turns back on
itself to D but drops to C♮ in a moment that suggests the sort of
modulation that Schubert made so much his own. Compare
Exx. 43 and 53 closely in terms of *sound* and you will appreciate
the emotional change which this seemingly simple modification
brings about.

continuing in
F major

Always up to now the curious C♯ has suggested that the music
was going to modulate, though quite in what direction it was
difficult to see; each time, Beethoven has sternly drawn it back

towards the home key of E♭ major. This time he allows it to have
its head and the feeling of release is almost physical.

The Recapitulation is by no means exact; page after page reveals
new touches to the attentive ear, until the movement ends with
a coda[1] of quite extraordinary richness—so much so that it seems
almost like a new development section. Very often the demarca-
tion of the coda or codetta from its preceding music seems a
matter of purely theoretical interest; here Beethoven gives us an
absolutely unmistakable sign that something of the greatest significance is still in store. Quite quietly the music comes to rest in the
tonic key of E♭ major. Then suddenly out of the blue comes an
immense chord of D♭, a tone lower, and still a shock even to ears
that have experienced Bartók and Stravinsky. In 1805 it must have
seemed an earthquake.

Ex.54

The dramatic effect is twofold, for not only are the swift and
unprepared changes of key from E♭ to D♭ and then to C major
immensely exciting, but their shock value is enhanced by sudden
alternations of *p*, *f*, *p*, and *ff*. Just as the audience is recovering its
breath, Beethoven sheds a totally unexpected light on the opening
theme by matching it to a positively skittish counter-melody.

This in turn leads to further new developments. Only by real

[1] See footnote, p. 13.

Ex.55

familiarity can one begin to appreciate the magnificent architecture of this great musical structure. It is an idealized conception of an anarchic society, where law, order, and unity are imposed from within, and not by the imposition of petty regulations from outside. To try to relate its purely musical form to worldly events is not merely imperceptive; it is an act of wilful misunderstanding; no events of ordinary life could change from one mood to another with such startling rapidity without making us all end up in the madhouse. Yet such changes are perfectly rational in music since music obeys other laws, laws that can bring acceptance of what might seem inexplicable in any other terms.

The second movement is a funeral march, but quite what Beethoven's motives were for electing to write one here I do not know. At a guess, I should say that it is merely a concession to the 'heroic' calibre of the music, in that heroes tend to be buried in pomp and ceremony; it would be unwise to assume that Beethoven was tactlessly anticipating Napoleon's funeral. There is even quite good evidence that the music was projected a couple of years earlier as a tribute to the English general, Sir Ralph Abercrombie, killed at the Battle of Alexandria in 1801. Composers are great opportunists, and it seems most likely that the incomplete march started on this earlier occasion gave Beethoven some material that came nicely to hand when he wanted it. So much for any relationship to a hard-and-fast programme.

Technically, one of the most interesting things in this movement is Beethoven's avoidance of drums at the beginning. With all their associations with military pomp, few composers could have resisted using them; instead he contents himself with low rumbles on the double basses, who here, most unusually for the

period, have a separate part from the 'cellos. Stripped of decorations, the first phrase of the funeral melody consists of the notes
G C E♭ C, which, for what it's worth, spell out the principal theme
of the first movement in the minor and backwards. This seems to
me to be no more than a happy coincidence calculated to excite
the musicological mind. So many classical themes are built on the
common chord that it would not be difficult to show a thematic
relationship between works separated from each other by
generations.

The immense span of the phrases in this movement and its slow
tempo mean that it is exceptionally long—too long for some, like
the man in the gallery at the first performance whom Czerny
heard moaning, 'I'd give a kreuzer if only it'd stop.' For those
who are prepared to adjust themselves to its measured tread there
are ample rewards, and a great deal more variety than one at first
realizes. Periodically the feeling of unalloyed grief is softened by
episodes like the one in C major in which the woodwind instruments commune together over a gentle murmuring of triplets
from the strings.

Structurally this is rather similar to the beautiful A major
clarinet tune in the middle of the slow movement of the Seventh
Symphony,[1] and such contrasts are like the warming rays of the
sun on a grey afternoon. Overall, the march leaves an impression
of profound grief, and again I would emphasize the stark impos-
sibility of devising a programme of Napoleonic episodes which
would fit both the death-like finality of this movement and the
immensely gay and vital scherzo which now follows. A much

[1] See p. 71.

more convincing and indeed brilliant elucidation of the 'programme' of the symphony has been suggested by J. W. N. Sullivan in his penetrating study of Beethoven's spiritual development.[1] He sees the 'Eroica' as a 'transcription of personal experience'. The first movement shows Beethoven's courage and defiance of fate; the second, the deep despair which his deafness had brought on, and to which I have already referred; the Scherzo celebrates the tremendous uprising of creative energy which the composer had experienced as he emerged from his own private hell, and of which the brilliant Second Symphony is a vivid reminder. In the finale, the choice of variation form symbolizes the range of achievement which is now open to the 'Promethean' energy of the reawakened spirit. This analysis seems to me both psychologically sound and musically convincing; it changes the 'programme' of the symphony to the musical exposition of general states of mind—which is precisely the sort of thing which music can do successfully. When it comes to illustrating actual events it is far less happy, unless a written catalogue of what it is supposed to be representing is supplied. We accept an atmospheric image of the sea in Debussy's *La Mer*; we can appreciate the difference between the Swan and the Asses in *The Carnival of the Animals*; but the intelligent mind revolts at the thought of the first movement of the 'Eroica' representing Napoleonic squadrons of cavalry; Beethoven's only attempt at such pictorialism, in the 'Battle' symphony, was a foregone disaster.

A scherzo such as we now find was a form virtually invented by Beethoven, of which this is the first outstanding example. Admittedly the corresponding movement in the second symphony has many points of originality, and speaks to us in an idiom that goes beyond the resources of Mozart or Haydn. Remarkable though it is, it still remains light-weight; in comparison, the 440 bars of the 'Eroica' scherzo seem to establish a new conception of the permissible scale for such a movement. The classic Menuet and Trio from which the scherzo form was

[1] J. W. N. Sullivan: *Beethoven*: William Brown and Co., 1927.

derived has now receded so far into the background that it is
completely forgotten.

The movement begins with a quiet and excited bustle on the
strings out of which emerges a tune of infectious gaiety played by
the first violins doubled at the upper octave by a solo oboe.
Despite the fact that the piece is in E♭ major, this vital theme
appears in B♭, an unexpected twist which obviously caused
Beethoven considerable head-scratching, since his first sketches all
indicate that the melody should be in the tonic key of E♭. It is
interesting to compare his first version with the one we now
know. Here is the preliminary sketch:

Ex.57

and it breaks off there.

The presence of an A♮ in the third full bar shows that his mind
was already veering towards the dominant key of B♭, since A♮
is the essential modulating note that will take us from E♭ major
to B♭ major. Where this sketch shows a weakness, which
Beethoven subsequently rectified, is in its initial departure on a
journey which is too soon contradicted by a return home. If you
play the example above and then immediately compare it with
the final version below, you will realize the superiority of
Beethoven's revision, since once it has set out towards B♭ major
it avoids the tame return to E♭ and states the tune clearly in the
new key regardless of academic sanction.

Ex.58

This wisp of melody flits bat-like through the score; the volume remains at a low level in spite of the gaiety of the music.

At one point, Beethoven twists the tail of the principal theme by detaching the last four bars of the example above and playing tag with them through the orchestra.

At last, with a great thump of timpani and a blare of brass, the whole band come sweeping in with the main theme—the justification for this joyful noise being that it is the first time that the theme has appeared in the home key of E♭. Over and over again one finds comparable passages in classical music which merely underline the importance of the key system; a tonality lost leads to passages of vagueness and mystery, a tonality rediscovered is greeted with acclamation and triumph. Had Beethoven retained his first sketch for this movement (see Ex. 57) he would have deprived himself of the musical justification for this exciting climax. The effect of jubilation is all the greater in that the orchestra appear to be tumbling over themselves with excitement —so much so that the theme overlaps itself, like voices babbling in a crowd.

Momentarily, the strings stand clear from the ruck, and a new theme marked by strong off-beat accents impresses itself on our memories.

Ex.61

Much has been made of the possible relationship between this and the initial theme of the first movement,[1] but I feel it is unlikely to be anything more than a subconscious reflection. When Beethoven does use cyclic unity of this kind, as for instance he does when he makes the scherzo theme of the Fifth Symphony reappear in the finale, he generally makes his intentions pretty clear. If you consider the state of a composer's mind when creating a work on this scale, it is only natural that all sorts of related themes should be swirling about in his brain at one and the same time. So tempestuous a movement as the first allegro of this symphony must have given him many a sleepless night, and its patterns would have sunk so deeply into his subconscious that it is small wonder if they have influenced subsequent passages. Commentators who greet the theme above as a deliberate reference to the first movement conveniently ignore the striking difference it makes when Beethoven subsequently changes its rhythm to duple time—an ingenious way of making an apparent *accelerando*.

Ex.62

It would seem to be far more likely that Beethoven was consciously trying to *avoid* any suggestion of the first movement, since he rejected a theme for the Trio which does certainly have both melodic and rhythmic similarities. Of the four or five sketches he made for the middle section of this great scherzo, the first bears a strong resemblance to the 'cello tune from the opening allegro.

[1] See p. 52, Ex. 43.

Ex.63

Even allowing for the fact that the choice of notes here is to a certain extent dictated by what was comfortable for a horn to play, the first two bars of this example do seem to be suspiciously close to the first bars of the opening theme. Surely then Beethoven's total rejection of this idea indicates his distaste for such a relationship. Instead, we find the three horns embarking on a theme which is still built on the 'common chord' of Eb major out of practical necessity,[1] but which goes out of its way to avoid any suggestion of earlier material.

Ex.64

Where this Trio is remarkable is in the increasingly poetic element which it introduces; it is the epitome of that peculiarly German romanticism which we find so often in the music of Schumann and Wagner, and this is perhaps its first expression.

The *pp* start of the movement makes the return to the opening material a comparatively simple matter; a last sigh from the horns recedes into a twilight stillness, and then once again the strings (but this time reduced in numbers by the elimination of second violins and violas) bring us back to the bustle and gaiety with which the movement had begun.

Ever since the first performance of the 'Eroica', the Finale has been the movement most open to criticism. In part, this may have been due to the overall dimensions of the work, which far exceed those of any earlier symphony; performances were even given omitting the Scherzo and Finale, and a characteristic example of

---

[1] The horn in Beethoven's time had no valves, and in consequence could only play the 'harmonic series'; for further explanation see any musical dictionary.

critical acumen was displayed in a London magazine called the *Harmonicon*, which in its April issue of 1829 said that 'if this symphony is not by some means abridged, it will soon fall into disuse'. In fact, it is difficult to visualize any alternative form for this finale, except possibly a fugue. Drama and fantasy have had their say in the first movement, grief and pathos in the second, gaiety and high spirits in the third; the one notable omission has been what might be termed the 'craft' element in composition. Obviously, enormous skill has been displayed throughout, but not of the conscious kind that the writing of a fugue or set of variations involves. In the event, Beethoven decided to elaborate a theme which must have been an especial favourite, since he had already used it in his 'Prometheus' ballet-music, and also as the basis for the Op. 35 piano variations. It is just possible that there may have been some subtle connection in his mind between the 'heroic' aspect of Napoleon and the legendary figure of Prometheus, though I tend to believe that by the time he reached this movement, thoughts of Napoleon had become a very minor consideration, so deeply would he have been involved in a purely musical conception.

He begins with a torrent of semiquavers which may well have been in the back of Tchaikovsky's mind when he came to write the finale of his Fourth Symphony; but whereas Tchaikovsky's passage suggests a Bacchanale, this obviously presages something of a highly serious nature. An impressive pause leads us to a quiet and positively skeletonic statement of the 'Prometheus' theme on *pizzicato* strings.

Ex.65

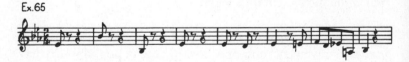

To describe this as the 'Prometheus' theme is misleading—as misleading as Beethoven is (deliberately) in suggesting that we are now hearing a tune on which variations are to be built.

What he has done is the equivalent of starting a set of variations on 'God Save the King' with *pizzicato* 'cellos and basses doing this:

Ex. 66

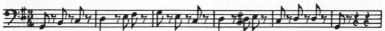

In other words, what we have heard is not a theme, but the *bass* of a theme, and its elevation to the status of a melody is typical of Beethoven's dry humour.[1] Strings and woodwind proceed to play Grandmother's Footsteps with this undistinguished-looking fragment; there is a silence of three beats, and then an apparently inexplicable outburst of three explosive B flats on full wind, brass, and timpani. Another silence, and then a quiet sustained B♭, as if these rowdy intruders were apologizing for their bad manners. However, after four more bars of decorum, the heckling begins again; this time even the strings are infected, and the same explosions occur, together with a similar apology.

On the face of it, this is sheer madness on Beethoven's part. It is, of course, an elaborate trick; a fair comparison would be the schoolboy joke relating to this picture:

The viewer is supposed to make several fruitless guesses as to the subject, whereupon the artist, falling about with mirth, reveals that it is a giraffe walking past a window. Judging from his music, this would have convulsed Beethoven; for in just the same way, what he has done here is to give us a suggestion of an outline without any of the vital details. He prolongs the suspense still further by embarking on two quite orthodox variations on what we have heard so far; we are even ready to believe that this

---

[1] It is curious that none of our more 'psychological' critics has suggested that this promotion of a simple bass line to melodic status *might* be a symbolic representation of the improved lot of the post-Revolutionary French worker. . . .

skeleton of a theme is the real thing, and that the B♮ outbursts are
mere eccentricity. Then comes the revelation; at last we see that
the picture wasn't a complete picture at all, but only a part of it.
The presumptuous bass takes its proper place, like a servant that
has been caught trying on his master's clothes; for the first time
we hear the true melody which had been in Beethoven's mind the
whole time. Put *with* the bass, like this, all becomes clear, and the
loud B flats followed by the 'apology' fall into perspective.

So breathtaking a revelation is naturally greeted with a good
deal of excitement by the orchestra, and there is a fair amount of
running hither and thither before the music settles down to a
serious discussion of the now fully comprehended material. Since
the practical jokes are over, and a serious fugue is about to be
launched, the key very properly turns to the more severe climate
of C minor. Thus modified, the 'bass' which has so misled us takes
on new stature, and we at once respond to the change of mood.

This is worked out in ever-increasing complexity and animation, until the 'Prometheus' melody unexpectedly reappears in the
wildly remote key of B minor. This in turn is varied in the woodwind, while the first violins have a scampering phrase that suggests
the sort of frenzied activity which we associate today with 'novelty'
pieces with names like 'Toboggan-run' or 'Holiday on Wheels'.
It would be wearisome to chronicle each appearance of the theme
from now on; suffice it to say that either the 'bass' or the 'melody'
of the theme is never far away. The main scheme of things is a
skilful alternation of fugal sections with more openly dramatic
chordal writing. By avoiding committing himself to a strict fugue
Beethoven has the best of both worlds; he can demonstrate his
craftsmanship in some pages while being free to indulge in
dramatics when he wishes.

Perhaps the greatest surprise still to come is the central change
of tempo, which is prepared as though it were a cadenza in a
concerto. In a way, it *is* a cadenza—a cadenza for composer, for
now Beethoven seems to embark on a glorious improvisation, in
which the 'Prometheus' melody assumes new beauty by being
slowed to an Andante. Cadenza-like, this section surveys the
material of the movement and treats it with a new freedom; the
rigours of counterpoint are forgotten in passages of great harmonic richness. At last the music settles on to a long-reiterated
G in the 'cellos, over which curiously alternating harmonies
chatter quietly in woodwind and strings; and then, like a sudden
door thrown open letting in a blast of cold air, the same cascade
of notes with which the movement had begun sweeps us back into
a final tumultuous Presto.

So enormous an advance over its predecessors does this work
reveal in idiom, in technique, and in the whole conception of what

music was capable of expressing, that we cannot be surprised that it caused perplexity and hostility in many listeners before it finally established itself as one of the great landmarks of music. After its first performance it was described in the *Allgemeine Musikalische Zeitung* as

> a lengthy, wild and bold fantasy, most difficult to perform. While there is no lack of strikingly beautiful sections in which one can discern the energy and talent of the composer, the work often strays into utter irregularity . . . there is too much that is shrill and bizarre . . . one almost entirely loses any sense of coherence.

Other critics took Beethoven to task for not continuing the style of his early works. One criticism strikes a very familiar note: it expresses a fear lest music should become so complex that it will become the exclusive preserve of the expert, and that the ordinary listener will leave the concert-hall depressed by incoherent and overblown ideas as well as by the perpetual noise of the full orchestra.[1] How many times through the centuries have these words been spoken about 'contemporary' music?

[1] See Max Graf: *Composer and Critic*: Chapman & Hall 1947.

CHAPTER V

BEETHOVEN

Symphony No. 7 in A major, Op. 92 (1812)

1. Poco sostenuto, leading to Vivace. 2. Allegretto. 3. Scherzo; presto. 4. Finale; allegro con brio.

Orchestra: 2 flutes; 2 oboes; 2 clarinets; 2 bassoons; 2 horns; 2 trumpets; 2 timpani; normal complement of strings.

Notice the return to only two horns, compared with the three in the 'Eroica'. Normally, Beethoven is quite content with two; the Third (3) and Ninth (4) symphonies are the sole examples of his demanding more. There is a gap of over three years between this symphony and its predecessor, No. 6 (Op. 68). There is no particular reason for this except that he had a slight tendency to write works in pairs; thus we find symphonies No. 5 and 6 are Op. 67 and Op. 68. So great an effort of concentration on the largest orchestral form probably made him turn to other fields until the next impulse, which produced No. 7 (Op. 92) and No. 8 (Op. 93).

IN HIS SEVENTH SYMPHONY Beethoven returns to the old classical device of a slow introduction; he had already used this in his First, Second, and Fourth Symphonies, and in a way it is a little surprising to find what would appear to be a retrograde step as late as Op. 92. A comparison with these earlier works is revealing, however, since it shows us how his sense of architectural scale was developing. In the First Symphony the slow introduction is a scant twelve bars; in the Second, we find this nearly trebled to thirty-three bars; the proportions of the Fourth are much the same—thirty-eight bars, but by the time we reach the Seventh Symphony, the introduction takes on the importance of an annexe rather than an entrance since it is no less than sixty-two bars long. When you consider that the entire slow movement of the 'Pathétique' Sonata is a mere seventy-three bars of Adagio 2/4, and that here we have sixty-two bars of 4/4 (twice the length of bar, even if at a slightly quicker tempo), you begin to realize quite how Beethoven's conception of the overall proportions of a movement had changed.

There are many points of originality in this opening. The one that attracts immediate attention is the scoring of the first few bars. Beethoven begins with a full chord, using the entire orchestra including a forte stroke on the drum. Out of this there emerges the only sustained note, on a single oboe—a dramatic contrast indeed. Every 'odd' bar on the first page has a similar explosive chord, but all the way through they are joined to each other by slender strands of woodwind, as though great pillars had decorative ropes connecting them. In each gap we find more voices progressively joining in; the first link is for solo oboe, the next for oboe and clarinet; then four instruments take up the refrain—flute, oboe, clarinet, and horn, so that one has a wonderful sense of some musical ritual in which the instruments take their places according to an ancient preordained pattern. This is true architecture in terms of sound, since it can easily be indicated in visual symbols.

Ex.69

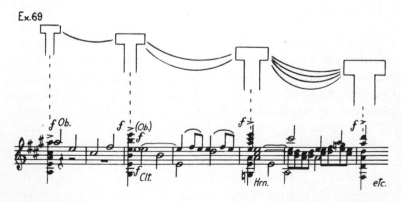

Beethoven may have felt that there was a danger that these long

arches of sound might be too great in their span for easy comprehension; so, still keeping the same majestic pace, he now helps us
across the chasms by quicker moving notes which carry the ear
from point to point with greater ease. Once he has accustomed us
to this new development, he returns to the first idea; but this time,
what had been a mere sketch has the details filled in. We still find
the same steps from pillar to pillar; there is a tremendous difference
in the effect, though, for around these striding notes there bustles
a multitude of semiquavers. A glance at bars 15-22 of the score
will show at once what I mean.

Unexpectedly, the music suddenly begins to quieten; the scales
disperse into thin air and the woodwind introduce a theme which
suggests a march, but again a march of a curiously ritual quality,
as though it belonged to a temple rather than a parade-ground.
Its feeling of remoteness is intensified by the tonality of C major
in which we now find ourselves. This is foreign territory indeed,
and part of our interest must be in waiting to see how Beethoven
is going to get back. In a 'thriller', one is kept in a state of suspense
wondering how the hero is going to get out of a tight situation;
this might be termed a celestial equivalent, since the musician will
not only have realized the strange world that the music has
entered, but will also be absorbed in observing its return to the
familiar pastures of A major.

The strings take up the march theme in their turn, while oboe
and bassoon keep nagging away at a G natural—which only serves
to underline our remoteness from the home key, since the most
essential note to establish the key of A major is a G sharp. Then,
with increasing excitement, Beethoven seems to see the way back.
Here is a simplified skeleton which shows the various stepping-
stones that he uses.

Ex.70 Quite slow

Ex. 70 *cont.*

Once again it seems a suitable moment to stress the point already made on p. 63; the crescendo here springs not from any desire on Beethoven's part to illustrate some external excitement; it arises purely because the home key of A major has at last been sighted. The last two chords of Ex. 70 show how he has the tonality of A in his grasp; indeed, a lesser composer would probably have been quite content to have accepted the ending I have suggested in brackets, albeit somewhat decorated. Where Beethoven reveals a master-stroke of genius is that with his goal so nearly reached, and with the knowledgeable listener about to sit back and relax, he pushes on recklessly and launches out into even more obscure keys. Instinct and training tell us that an arrival at this chord of the dominant must be the ultimate solution; by postponing it still further, Beethoven is like an author who rescues his hero from one predicament, only to pitch him into another. The laws of musical symmetry and tonal relationships are such that we can say that if a classical symphony has a slow introduction in a particular key, the chances are 99 in 100 that the main part of the movement will be in the same key. Every deviation from that key has the effect of putting off our arrival at what we can be virtually certain is our final destination.

Brushing aside the obvious, Beethoven drags us on by means of the same giant pillars with which we are already familiar. The quiet march theme returns again, this time in F major;[1] a comparable crescendo to the one quoted in Ex. 70, but with an element of increased tension, finally explodes into a gigantic E natural. For the second time we are in sight of the homeland. There ensues a passage which only goes to emphasize the rightness of

[1] It is worth checking the relative 'distances' of these keys on the housing estate plan on p. 19.

treating music as a language with its own rules, rather than as a mere translation of non-musical events into sound. I have laid enormous emphasis on keys in this analysis; how else can we explain the passage that now confronts us, in which Beethoven repeats the note E over seventy times in ten bars? At this point, he is playing with us. Already he has snatched us away from our ultimate goal of A major; now he keeps us in suspense a new way. 'Are you quite certain we've really made it this time?' he seems to say; and he goes on harping on this one note, teasing us with it, until at last he relents and goes skipping off into one of the happiest themes he ever thought of.

Nothing could more graphically illustrate the increased pleasure that an understanding of musical structure brings than this introduction. On the face of it, these fifteen pages of score are not particularly exciting; the music is slow, but without the compensation of any especially beautiful melody; it has a number of scales traipsing up and down, and several passages where Beethoven flogs one note to death. It would be easy to dismiss it as boring, and to the untrained ear it may well be so. To a musician, as I have tried to show you, it is a whole series of carefully planned moves towards or away from an ultimate destination. Far from merely juggling with tunes and colours and chords, the composer is combining an architect's vision with the campaigning sense of a general,[1] plus, at one point, a conjuror's deception. You can compare music with many other things, but in the long run it boils down to something which cannot be expressed except by the notes themselves. To interpret it entirely in emotional terms, as so many genuine lovers of music tend to do, is to reduce it to the level of a drug. Loud, quick music stimulates; quiet, slow music relaxes. If this were the whole story, what a petty art it would be; such aspects are only the superficialities, as inadequate as it would be to describe a sunset as 'red', or Michelangelo's David as 'a stone man'. Every sound induces an emotional response, even the distant hoot of a train whistle or the cosy clink

[1] Beethoven once said, 'If I knew as much about war as I do about music I could defeat Napoleon himself.'

of a teacup. In music, powerful though the emotional stimulus may be, it is often only a side-effect; the essential difference between so-called Classical and Romantic music lies in the change of balance between form and emotion. Classical music generates emotion from the abstract contemplation and manipulation of form; Romantic music is an expression of personal emotions translated into sound. The misunderstanding arises when people try to interpret music in the wrong terms by expecting to find similar beauties in a Bach fugue and a Chopin nocturne. Both are beautiful but in a totally different way, just as Shakespeare differs from Browning, or Corot from Franz Hals. What we have to learn is sufficient understanding of style and idiom to be able to appreciate the many worlds of music, and not to attempt to force it into our own narrow conception of what is beautiful or proper.

Once Beethoven is launched into the main part of the movement it is all fairly plain sailing. The music is for the most part extrovert and full of good humour. The principal theme is first presented on woodwind, which gives it a suitably pastoral flavour.

Ex.71

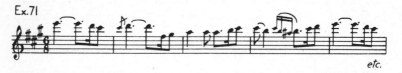

etc.

The strings seem to take a little while to cotton on to this new mood, and several times they question the woodwind with this interrogatory phrase:

Ex.72

Ultimately they gain confidence, and join in with an enthusiastic rush of semiquavers while 'cellos and basses drum approvingly below.

Particular mention should be made of the variation of tone in this score; seldom before has Beethoven combined such happiness of mood with such violent and arresting changes from loud to soft. The dangers of an excess of rum-ti-tum which sometimes become so apparent in this type of bucolic music are skilfully avoided by the use of unpredictable dynamic marks.[1]

The second subject group is reached with the minimum of formality, and proves to be mainly concerned with two ideas, of which the first is of an unselfconscious singing quality that we normally might only expect to find in Schubert.

Ex.73

The second of these two elements preserves something of the rhythmic character of the first subject, but also introduces a brief but lyrical phrase on the strings by way of contrast.

Ex.74 W.W.

The end of the exposition and its subsequent join into the development section show us a lovely example of Beethoven's humour at its most slapstick. The closing bars of the exposition consist of a rising scale played as though the strings all had their gloves on, alternating with explosive off-beat E's from the wood-wind and brass, who, to use an Americanism in its literal sense, can't seem to get 'with it'.

Ex.75

---

[1] The technical term for f, p, ff, mf, etc.

This total lack of symphonic decorum prompts the two bars of stunned silence before the double bar. Assuming that we have done the repeat of the exposition, we now find the orchestra ploughing blindly on, only to come to an abrupt halt.

Ex. 76

This second silence provokes the question, 'And where do you think we're going to now?' Observe that this apparent violence is not to be taken seriously; this is the roar of father pretending to be a lion, not the storm and anguish we find in the Fifth or Ninth symphonies. As though entering into the spirit of the game, the violins ever so tentatively suggest that since the whole thing seems to have broken down completely, the only thing to do is to go back to something familiar and start again. Gradually the other sections of the orchestra join in, although still in a very subdued mood after the 'disgrace' of the preceding two examples.

The danger of using a simile such as comparing music to father pretending to be a lion is that it plants an inflexible picture in people's minds. While I am convinced that at that particular moment Beethoven was suggesting a mood of boisterous knock-about humour which can be compared to such domestic larks, music is such a fantastic and unique world that it can translate us from this mood to another infinitely remote in a matter of seconds. It may be all right to see father on his hands and knees wearing the rug at one point, but it is absolutely fatal to look for him anywhere else in the movement. We must always be ready for some purely musical miracle that will lift us back into a more ethereal world. Here, for instance, is Beethoven charging happily along in E major:

Ex. 77

Having arrived triumphantly on this final E, and with such assurance that we feel we are bound to stay there for several pages, he whips round and shoots us into the totally unexpected key of C♯ major.

Ex. 78   W.W.(col 8ᵛᵃ)   (col 8ᵛᵃ)

Str
(col 8ᵛᵃ)   Actually E♯ but written
as F♮ for convenience

The sudden quietness of the sustained wind chord at the end is magical. Now it is just possible that a lesser composer might have got this far, and were he to have done so, we could predict that having reached this new tonal centre of D♭ major (or C♯—they are interchangeable), he would stay in it for at least a while. Beethoven is more subtle; he has yet another switch that catches us right off our guard. At the very instant that the woodwind confirm that departure from E major, just as we get our breath back from the shock, he gives the harmony still another twist and goes to an even more remote key. Go straight from the preceding example into this one and you will see what a striking change this new departure is.

Ex. 79   *
                                              etc.

* Passages like this appear to have had a particularly strong influence on Schumann.

This heart-stopping moment has the same sort of perfection as an impossible return in a tennis-match, or an effortless leg-glide from a ball you were sure had the batsman beaten. Since it is music, however, it is transient beauty made permanent.

One more delightful trap is worth mentioning before we leave this exhilarating movement. It concerns the blustering scale which ends the exposition (p. 77, Ex. 75). Some thirty-five pages later this same scale reappears in identical form, except that it is now in A instead of E. In every respect, the layout is exactly similar —the same fumble-fingered splodges on the strings, the same off-beat squeals from the woodwind, even down to the same two-bar silence. With the memory of the previous version in our minds, we sit there confidently expecting four more bomps and then a silence, out of which will emerge the violins *pp*. Once again Beethoven proves himself a master of the prepared surprise; instead of the awaited four loud notes he gives us one tentative and apologetic little peep from the strings, followed by an equally unnerved squeak from the wind. After a further silence, it is the 'cellos who this time restore order; we in the audience have been bamboozled on every point, and it is game, set, and match to Beethoven.

The second movement was an instant success. Whereas some critics were baffled by the first and last movements,[1] everyone loved the simplicity of the Allegretto. So much so that it was often taken out of its context and played in place of the slow movement of the Second Symphony, which was considered rather long and dreary. The composer's scheme in this movement is to present a tune that is more a sequence of chords than a melody, and then to enrich it by adding a warm and melting counter-tune. Too long to give in full in an essay such as this, I merely quote a few bars, with the counter-melody above:

[1] In Leipzig they said it could only have been composed when Beethoven was either ill or drunk, and Weber said the composer must now be ripe for the madhouse.

Ex. 80

By writing the melody of the third and seventh bars in the way he has, Beethoven has provided conductors and orchestral players with enough food for argument to keep them happy for years. Should the rhythm be played ♫♩♫♫, and if so why didn't he write it like that? Or did he want the first two notes to be sneaked in at the end of the previous bar? Or should they be quicker than written: ♫♩♫♫ ? For what it's worth, my own contribution to the debate would be this.

The Elizabethan name for an ornament was a 'relish'; nothing could more aptly convey the true function of ornamentation in music. It is a means of bestowing a special favour on the following note, of picking it out from its neighbours. By electing to write these two notes in an obsolescent form of notation, Beethoven was indicating not *when* they should be played but *how* they should be played—with a special affection, leading to an intensified pathos on the D. Since he was harking back to the period of his youth at this point by reviving a custom that was falling into disuse, it would seem most likely that the notes should be played with and not before the beat, as his father must have told him many a time in the unhappy music-lessons of his boyhood.

The movement is pervaded throughout by the solemn rhythmic pattern we find in each pair of bars in Ex. 80. Its constant reiteration has a hypnotic effect, but in itself this rhythm is without tenderness or compassion. Only when it is illuminated by the

counter-melody does it show any warmth. It is *Fidelio* all over
again, with the prisoners trudging hopelessly around the prison-
yard, only to find their misery evaporating beneath the healing
rays of the sun. Indeed in this movement the sun does shine with the
radiantly beautiful clarinet tune which appears half-way through.

Ex.81

p dolce

etc.

With an accompaniment of gently murmuring triplets from
the first violins we hardly notice the persistent trudge of the ♩ ♫
rhythm which still continues beneath. Beautiful though it is, this
melody does not succeed in dispelling the prevailing gloom, and
after a mere thirty-seven bars it is displaced by stern triplets which
cut descending swathes through the orchestra and herald the
return of the original material. This is treated in a slightly more
elaborate manner, including a ghostly little fugue; the sun comes
out once more in a brief memory of the clarinet tune before the
movement sinks once again into darkness. It ends as it had begun,
with a bleak A minor chord on the woodwind—two covers that
enclose this sad and brooding chapter.

It is easy to see why this movement has always been so popular;
its outlines are clear, its rhythm constant, its whole progress as
orderly as you could wish. The caprice and bluster of the first
movement have been replaced by the stylized pathos of a Greek
chorus, and this oasis of melancholy stillness, for all its sadness, was
welcomed by the puzzled audiences of the day.

The unpredictable Beethoven returns in the Scherzo, which is
full of practical jokes and a bustling animation which must have
seemed very regrettable to the older people in the concert-hall in
Vienna in 1814 when it was first performed. As the London
magazine *Harmonicon* said in July 1825, 'Beethoven's Seventh

Symphony is a composition in which the author has indulged in a great deal of disagreeable eccentricity. . . . We cannot discover any design in it, neither can we trace any connection in its parts. Altogether, it seems to have been intended as a kind of enigma —we had almost said a hoax.'[1]

When one listens to this splendid Scherzo with its extraordinary gaiety and vitality, it is almost incredible that any presumably intelligent connoisseur of music employed by a magazine devoted to musical topics should be able to deliver himself of such misguided rubbish. It is as well to remember, though, how unprepared the less perceptive members of a Beethoven audience were for the unconventionality of his music; where such reactions are still of value is in preventing us from becoming blasé about these compositions today. I would infinitely rather that someone was shocked by Beethoven's music than bored; at least to be shocked shows an awareness of the harmonic daring and formal enterprise that are to be found on nearly every page. Only by realizing the existence of such daring can we obtain the full savour of the excitement that is implicit in this score.

Once again, much of the drama is bound up in this question of tonality. The movement starts in a blustering and impatient mood, as though Beethoven were seizing the arpeggio of F major by the scruff of its neck.

Ex.82
Presto

In literally two seconds—which means in the next bar—and before the startled listeners have recovered from this aggressive battery, the mood changes to a nimble-footed dance. 'On the plains, fairy trains were a-treading measures,' says the madrigal; but Beethoven keeps not the dancers but the audience on the hop, for no sooner have we accustomed ourselves to this change of

[1] Quoted in Nicolas Slonimsky's brilliant and entertaining book, *Lexicon of Musical Invective*: Coleman-Ross: New York, 1953.

mood than he whips us into A major and causes the former bluster
to return. The statutory repeat of the first twenty-four bars only
serves to underline the conflict between these two opposing keys
of F and A, since the return to the beginning involves an abrupt
change from A major back to F major without any intervening
step. The second time round, we find the opening rhythm (shown
in the example above) being passed angrily from hand to hand in
the orchestra, like one of those party games where you have to
get rid of some object before the music stops.

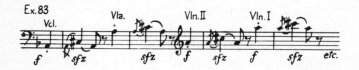

The next section is a typical example of how a classical composer plays with tonality. He has now firmly committed himself
to the sharp keys, and for a moment or two the woodwind chatter
away quite happily. Suddenly aware of how far they are away
from home, the strings, like anxious children, begin to wonder
how they can ever get back—home being F major. After all, here
they are in a key which contradicts the very essence of F, since the
F is sharpened.

It is the wiser heads in the orchestra who suggest a solution,
although they don't seem any too sure of it; tentatively the lower
instruments—bassoons, horn, 'cellos, and basses—suggest wiping
out this difficult 'sharp' element altogether.

Ex. 85

As you can see, there isn't even time for these lower voices to echo the four-times-repeated pattern previously established by the violins before the whole orchestra come in with an enthusiastic shout of 'That's it!' However, it isn't 'it'—not yet, that is to say; but it is a step in the right direction since it has at least got rid of the 'sharp' element. Beethoven now repeats this whole process, thus bringing him through C to B♭ major. Notice the instinctive sense of balance a composer of this period has; so far, the music has veered between F major and the sharp keys to the right of it on the 'housing estate'.[1] Now he compensates for that by a swing to the left; only by introducing more 'flat-ness' into the harmonic scheme can he finally restore the music convincingly to its original key.

The central Trio is exceptionally long, and seems a breath of calm after the explosive vitality that has preceded it. It is based on an old Pilgrims' Hymn which Beethoven came across and happily plundered. As if to emphasize that the hide-and-seek with tonality is over, the violins sustain an almost continuous A, while beneath, the woodwind gently sing their soothing phrases in D major. This reveals an interesting point about the conflicting tonalities of the movement. The note A is in fact a central pivot, and this whole Scherzo is concerned with three harmonizations of A.

Ex. 86

[1] See p. 19, Fig. 4.

This means that the first part of the Scherzo is a ding-dong struggle between 1 and 2, while the Trio is a period of respite on 3.

A rough idea of just how far the form of the Scherzo had progressed in importance in Beethoven's hands can be gained by comparing this symphony with the Second. In the earlier work, the Scherzo consists of seven pages of score, of which the first five are repeated, making twelve in all. In the Seventh Symphony, the Scherzo is fifty-seven pages long; what is more significant, the tempo varies noticeably from section to section, and not only in the usual central Trio. The plan is much more complex, since we now find scherzo-trio-scherzo-trio-scherzo, while on the final page there is a last four-bar remembrance of the Trio before the full orchestra impatiently cut in and bring the movement to an abrupt end.

It is curious that we tend to think of this symphony as a rather pastoral, almost light-weight affair when it is not only one of the largest in scale, but also the most extrovert in its boisterous good spirits. The finale bursts at the seams with good humour; Wagner described it as the 'Apotheosis of the Dance', but this is misleading in so far as it suggests the refinement of the ballet rather than the improvised steps of a group of slightly tipsy peasants at a country inn. Unquestionably there is urban music and rural music, two main streams that it is not too far-fetched to suggest stem from the opposing figures of Mozart and Haydn. Mozart has the polish and the sophistication, Haydn the direct and friendly manner. Mozart never gives you the man-to-man dig in the ribs that Haydn will, and of the two composers, Haydn was the more potent an influence on Beethoven. Such an influence is particularly vivid in this movement, with its driving rhythm and robust humour.

As is quite often the case, the Finale is in fairly normal sonata form, but with an enormously extended coda, which as an epilogue balances the lengthy prologue with which the work had begun. The start, needless to say, is yet another joke; Beethoven begins with an extremely positive assertion of E major tonality, only to modify it a couple of beats later, as if a speaker were to say, 'Ladies and gentle-creatures. . . .' Here is no gentleness, though, but a play on harmonies as my suggested address is a play on words.

Ex.87

If you try the experiment of staying in E major for a little longer on the lines suggested below, and then return to the symphony, you will regain the sensation of slight dislocation which Beethoven intended you to experience in the third bar.

Ex.88

A harmony teacher will probably dismiss this argument as nonsense, pointing out that the opening chord is not E major at all, but the dominant of A. I have learnt not to quarrel with theoreticians since the law is always on their side; my reply to the academic approach is to paraphrase the missionary's classic riposte: 'You continue to look at Beethoven your way and I will continue to look at him in his.' Not for a moment would I deny that the opening chord is the dominant; the point at issue is that Beethoven clearly wants you to be gulled into believing that it is the tonic —or to be less technical, E major.

The first subject material is divided into two basic ideas, one of which keeps chasing its tail:

Ex. 89

while the other is made of solid stuff.

Ex. 90

The second subject flirts incessantly with C♯ minor, but seldom commits itself to actually settling there; again the Schumannesque quality of the dotted rhythms is noticeable. Such is the driving force of the music, however, that there is little time to absorb detailed impressions, and Beethoven hurries us on with scant regard for subtlety. Worth noticing is a sudden patch of quiet writing in which he skilfully extends the last bar of Ex. 89, passing the little rising sixth through the whole range of the strings.

Ex. 91

This quieter section is only a brief respite, and in less than a minute we are pitched back into the full hurly-burly of the opening material.

The coda is characterized by a curious marching bass which anticipates the type of figure we might expect to find in a symphony by Sibelius. High sustained chords in the woodwind impose some cohesion on the breathless snatches of semiquavers which scud through the violins and violas, while below, 'cellos and basses grind uneasily like the tremor of an earthquake.

Gradually over this disturbed bass line there accumulates an increasing intensity of sound, building remorselessly until in blazing triumph the opening material of the movement returns. For Beethoven to use the *fff* sign is rare indeed and one of its few appearances is in these closing pages. Rare also are any opinions he ever gave about his own music, but of this work he makes brief mention in two of his letters. In both he refers to it as 'one of my best works'. What more is there to add?

CHAPTER VI

BERLIOZ

Symphonie Fantastique, Op. 14 (1830)

Sub-title: 'An episode in the life of an artist.' Berlioz himself supplied the extensive programme note quoted below:[1]

PROGRAMME OF THE SYMPHONY

A young musician of unhealthily sensitive nature and endowed with vivid imagination has poisoned himself with opium in a paroxysm of love-sick despair. The narcotic dose he had taken was too weak to cause death, but it has thrown him into a long sleep accompanied by the most extraordinary visions. In this condition his sensations, his feelings, and memories find utterance in his sick brain in the form of musical imagery. Even the beloved one takes the form of melody in his mind, like a fixed idea which is ever returning and which he hears everywhere.

FIRST MOVEMENT: Visions and Passions (*Largo—piu mosso—allegro agitato e appassionato assai—religiosamente*)

At first he thinks of the uneasy and nervous condition of his mind, of sombre longings, of depression and joyous elation without any recognizable cause, which he experienced before the beloved one had appeared to him. Then he remembers the ardent love with which she suddenly inspired him; he thinks of his almost insane anxiety of mind, of his raging jealousy, of his reawakening love, of his religious consolation.

SECOND MOVEMENT: A ball (*Valse; allegro non troppo*)

In a ballroom, amidst the confusion of a brilliant festival, he finds the loved one again.

THIRD MOVEMENT: In the country (*Adagio*)

It is a summer evening. He is in the country musing when he

[1] English translation by Harry Brett; taken from the full orchestral score published by Breitkopf and Härtel, copyright 1900.

hears two shepherd-lads who play the *ranz des vaches* (the tune used by the Swiss to call their flocks together) in alternation. This shepherd duet, the locality, the soft whisperings of the trees stirred by the zephyr-wind, some prospects of hope recently made known to him, all these sensations unite to impart a long unknown repose to his heart and to lend a smiling colour to his imagination. And then she appears once more. His heart stops beating; painful forebodings fill his soul. 'Should she prove false to him?' One of the shepherds resumes the melody, but the other answers him no more. . . . Sunset . . . distant rolling of thunder . . . loneliness . . . silence.

FOURTH MOVEMENT: The procession to the stake (*Allegretto non troppo*)

He dreams that he had murdered his beloved, that he has been condemned to death and is being led to the stake. A march that is alternately sombre and wild, brilliant and solemn, accompanies the procession. . . . The tumultuous outbursts are followed without modulation by measured steps. At last the fixed idea returns; for a moment a last thought of love is revived—which is cut short by the death-blow.

FIFTH MOVEMENT: The witches' sabbath (*Larghetto; allegro*)

He dreams that he is present at a witches' dance, surrounded by horrible spirits, amidst sorcerers and monsters in many fearful forms, who have come to assist at his funeral. Strange sounds, groans, shrill laughter, distant yells, which other cries seem to answer. The beloved melody is heard again, but it has its noble and shy character no longer; it has become a vulgar, trivial, and grotesque kind of dance. SHE it is who comes to attend the witches' meeting. Friendly howls and shouts greet her arrival. . . She joins the infernal orgy . . . bells toll for the dead . . . a burlesque parody of the *Dies Irae* . . . the witches' round dance . . . the dance and the *Dies Irae* are heard at the same time.

Orchestra: 2 flutes; 2 oboes; 2 clarinets; 4 bassoons; 4 horns; 2 harps; 2 cornets; 2 trumpets; 3 trombones; 2 tubas; 5 or 6 percussion; strings, divided into nine parts in the finale, and having the double basses divided into four in the fourth movement.

The first movement is scored for a basic classical orchestra—
double woodwind, four horns, two trumpets, timpani, and
strings. The only unorthodox addition is a pair of cornets. The
two harps are added in the second movement only. In the
Adagio, the second oboe plays a cor anglais; the heavy extra brass
and percussion are kept in reserve for the last two movements.
The symphony was first performed in 1830 in Paris; Berlioz
revised it somewhat the following year and the work as we know
it now was given on 9 December 1832, two days before the
composer's twenty-ninth birthday. Originally the symphony was
intended to introduce a stage performance of a 'lyric mono-
drama' entitled *Lélio*, now forgotten.

PERHAPS THE MOST REMARKABLE thing about this literally
fantastic symphony is the date of its composition. At the time,
Schubert had been dead a scant eighteen months; Mendelssohn
was a youth of twenty-one, though an immensely talented one;
Schumann was just beginning to compose; Wagner was only
seventeen years old. This bare recital of facts may serve to bring
home quite how astoundingly original this somewhat despised
masterpiece is. It may have faults of taste and construction; it may
on occasion seem naïve or overblown; but whatever its weak-
nesses it remains a landmark in musical history, affirming the
liberation of music that Beethoven had initiated, and proclaiming
the new era of Romanticism, in which extravagant expression,
literary images, and personal feelings were to engulf the formality
of the classical age. Up to now, the conception of a symphony had
been almost entirely governed by what one might term architectural considerations. Even the slow movement of Beethoven's
'Pastoral' Symphony is not tied to any specific plot; Beethoven
himself warned us that we should regard the symphony more as
an impression of the countryside than as an actual painting.[1] As
opposed to this, Berlioz's approach was revolutionary; he had
clearly identified himself with the hero of De Quincey's *Confessions
of an Opium-eater*, which he had recently discovered in a rather
unreliable translation by Alfred de Musset. Interwoven with this

[1] 'Mehr Ausdruck der Empfindung als Mahlerei.'

romantic if unhealthy fantasy were all the torments of his love for Harriet Smithson, the Irish actress with whom he was infatuated, and whom he was later to marry disastrously. All the lurid details of this affair can be read in Berlioz's autobiography—one of the greatest and most revealing, not to say entertaining, life-stories ever written. There is no more vivid picture of artistic life in Paris in the mid-nineteenth century.[1]

No emotion in Berlioz's life could ever be simple or straight-forward, and his feelings for his Irish lady-love waxed and waned in a disturbingly inconsistent manner. In February 1830, while he was still working on the symphony, he wrote to a friend about his beloved. 'She is still in London,' he said, 'and yet I seem to feel her near me. All my former feelings for her are aroused, and combine to tear me to pieces; I hear my heart beat, and its pulsa-tions shake me as though they were the strokes of the piston-rod of a steam-engine.' (Not the most romantic of similes perhaps, but at least it had the merit of being up-to-date, since Stevenson's Rocket had first startled the world in the previous year.) One finds it hard to take such a passion seriously, however vehement Berlioz's words may have been, since at the time he had never even spoken to the fair Harriet, and his love was therefore exactly comparable to the crush a contemporary adolescent might have for a famous film-star. Only a few months after he had written the letter quoted above, disillusionment set in; for some reason never really elucidated, he conceived feelings of hatred and disgust for the unfortunate Miss Smithson, and this very work which had been planned as a tribute to her was to become a musical diatribe. In his original sketch of the programme for this symphony he described the last movement as 'a vision of a night of revelry'. There was no mention of witches; only when his love turned sour was the intended gaiety changed to a scene of horror.

It is possible that one reason for Berlioz's insistence on a literary 'programme' for the *Symphonie Fantastique* was that in his relative immaturity he did not feel confident enough to handle the

[1] *Memoirs of Hector Berlioz* edited by Ernest Newman: Tudor Publishing Co., New York, 1932.

variations of tempo in which he delights in the first movement
without some extra-musical justification. Beethoven had frequently
changed the tempo in his later works; instances such as the last
quartets or the Op. 109 piano sonata spring to mind. Whereas
Beethoven obviously regarded such changes as a logical musical
development, Berlioz may well have wanted to justify them by
some literary parallel. What is completely his own is something
that I can only describe as a purely physical rejoicing in sound for
sound's sake. This revelling in sonority was a totally new experience in music, all the more remarkable in a composer as sketchily
trained as Berlioz appears to have been.

In his elaborate programme note, Berlioz makes frequent mention of the fixed idea (*idée fixe*), or 'beloved' theme; this is a
lengthy musical phrase which is destined to appear in all five
movements. It is first suggested in the third bar, when, after a
brief woodwind introduction, the strings have a series of intensely
emotional phrases of which the first is the most important.

For the moment, however, we are not to know this; it is
enough to follow these languishing phrases, marvellously scored
as they are. Suddenly and surprisingly, the dark mood of this
opening is dissipated by gay fluttering figures on strings and
woodwind. We realize at once that we are in the presence of a
master of the orchestra. The mood continues to vacillate until the
music seems to be caught in some epileptic seizure; as though our
opium addict were gasping for breath, we find these extra-
ordinary markings on the score: | *mf dim.* > *pp* < *cresc.* | *ff ppp*
—this in a span of only two bars. The music quickens to a tempo
four times as fast in which, once established, the motto theme or
idée fixe makes its first complete appearance. It is sufficiently
important to quote in full.

Ex.94

Fast and passionate

By any standards this is an astonishing piece of music. One could easily criticize the tune itself for being too sequential, but criticism pales before the blazing intensity of its phrases, emphasized as they are by the extraordinary stabbing accents, the wild crescendi and diminuendi, and most of all, the thumping heart-beats beneath the spare and sinewy line of the melody. While it is not inconceivable that Wagner or Schumann might have written a theme on these lines, no one but Berlioz could have treated it in this way. Not until Stravinsky or Britten did anyone dare to orchestrate so uncompromisingly or to use rhythms as abrupt and independent as the ones we find in this accompaniment. No living soul could have taught Berlioz such orchestration or such har-mony, and this whole score shows a revolution in musical texture just as remarkable as the one that Beethoven had accomplished in form. His adoration for Beethoven and Gluck ensured that much of his music was a continuation of a tradition; despite his astonish-ing originality, he had no real wish to break the links with all that he valued from the past. He is like a gigantic stepping-stone, by whose means we can bridge the immense gulf between the classi-cal and modern periods; his flair was for invention, though, and the occasions when he does try to employ classical devices such as the fugue are usually the least satisfactory moments.

In itself the development of this lengthy theme is unremarkable as pure composition; it is the details that are exciting. Once the *idée fixe* has been fully stated, as in Ex. 94, the music goes tearing off into tempestuous blasts of sound, again alternating with strange pleading phrases on the woodwind. Fragments of the motto theme rush past, but there is little time to be aware of anything except the breathless pace of the music.

At the start of the development section proper—in so far as it is not fairly futile to force this work into the corset of normal symphonic form—'cellos and basses occupy themselves with the first few bars of the motto theme.

Ex.95

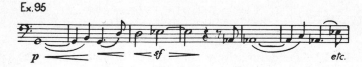

All thoughts of this material are soon forgotten, however, in

a passage which is a quite incredible anticipation of a technique
we associate most readily with Sibelius. The strings rise and fall
in wild chromatic eddies above which we hear the banshee cries
of the woodwind, like lost spirits driven before the whirlwind.
This terrifying passage explodes in a final dissonance, which is
followed by three bars of total silence, out of which emerges a
single *pp* horn note. Above this, the original theme reappears,
taking the limelight pretty extensively for the next few pages of
the score. Only a detailed study of these pages will show quite
how original Berlioz's conception is; compare any of them at
random with one of the Beethoven symphonies and you will
notice at once the far greater use of dynamics, the louds and softs,
the accents, changes of tempo, and so on. These are the superficial
differences; look then at the individual parts—the way he divides
'cellos from double basses, divides the basses themselves; observe
the detailed instructions to the percussion players. 'The first
quaver of each half-bar to be played with two drum-sticks; the
other five quavers with the right-hand drum-stick.' (Fourth
movement.) These are the sort of instructions we find in works by
Bartók or Villa-Lobos, not in composers of the eighteen-thirties.
Other passages show an uncanny prediction of twentieth-century
intervals. Play this sequence of notes slowly and ask any musical
friend what date he would estimate them to have been composed.

The likelihood of a right answer is exceedingly remote; they
occur in the last movement of this work.

Detailed thematic analysis of the type that is so fruitful in a
Beethoven symphony is of little value here; Berlioz's development of themes is easily grasped. What is infinitely more important is to be able to appreciate what I might term the 'flavour' of

the music; to be able to see in detail just how remarkable it is. From a spiritual standpoint the closing bars of the first movement are childish in their delineation of religious consolation. A few Amen-like chords on the orchestra do not begin to approach the profound depths that we find so often in Beethoven, Bach, and Mozart. To take Berlioz's programme at its face-value would be disastrous; it is thrilling enough to find a young man of twenty-seven daring so much. Let us not look for miracles by expecting him to match the fearlessness of his invention with the maturity of an older head.

The second movement begins with atmospheric rustlings which are particularly notable for the originality of the harp writing, an instrument which, without making any exhaustive research on the subject, I should say was appearing for the first time in a symphony. In due course an elegant waltz tune emerges, scored with characteristic delicacy. As a nice instance of Berlioz's delight in orchestral subtleties, look at what he can do with the 'pom-ching-ching' background that inevitably appears in every waltz. As a change from the eternal first beat on 'cellos and basses and the two subsequent beats on violas, second violins, and/or horns, he colours each quaver beat with a different section of the orchestra.

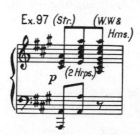

Meantime, the waltz tune weaves its way with the utmost clarity through this charmingly varied texture.

Suddenly a cold shiver seems to strike the onlookers, and over a quiet but excited *tremolando* in the strings the *idée fixe* is heard again, clearly recognizable, even if somewhat more suave than it has previously been.

Ex.98

A marvellous touch here is the immediate quickening of the pulse that Berlioz conveys when this theme now appears. Beneath the unruffled surface of the melody, which in its woodwind coloration seems as disdainful as a *Vogue* model, 'cellos and basses are given strange off-beat pulsations, perfectly transcribing the muted hammering in the unseen lover's ear as his blood quickens at the sight of his beloved.

Ex.99

In a moment we hear the waltz rhythm pick up, unperturbed by this little drama; the motto theme continues on its elegant way and passes from sight. Only near the end of the movement does it return; perhaps the young man sees his love climbing into her carriage; something certainly happens to disturb him, for this second apparition is greeted by a stormy outburst from the full orchestra. Unregarded in his isolation, he is quickly engulfed in a swirling cavalcade of dancers, and the movement ends in brilliance and gaiety.

The third movement begins with a pastoral dialogue between cor anglais and oboe. Berlioz's romantic imagination had been fired by the sound of Swiss peasants calling the cattle off the mountainside with some sort of pipe or horn. Typically he arranges for the oboe to play behind the stage, so as to give an effect of distance. To start with, these two instruments are un-accompanied, but after several interchanges, the softest possible tremor on violas and 'cellos begins, like a raincloud casting a dark streak across a pale summer sky. The mood is not unlike Words-worth—a somewhat idyllic conception of country life, but evocative for all that.

Violins and flute now introduce a new idea, one of Berlioz's curiously spare melodies. In his individual way he lets the tune speak for itself, stripped bare of all but the simplest harmonic suggestions,[1] so that when at last other instruments do appear one has a wonderful feeling of added richness. Much of this recalls the slow movement of Beethoven's 'Pastoral' Symphony, whose influence even goes so far as to suggest actual rhythmic patterns to Berlioz's ear. Over and over again the woodwind reiterate this figure, ♪♪, which is surely the cry of the quail in Beethoven's score. But while there are several such superficial resemblances, the orchestral texture is entirely different. Beethoven would never lay out a melody in the stark way that Berlioz does; nor did he ever devise a rhythm quite so intricate as the one we find a few pages further on at the next appearance of the motto theme. Again the tune is allotted to the woodwind, and the similarity of tonal colour to the ballroom version is obviously intended; but where before the reaction of 'cellos and basses was a quiet agitation (see Ex. 99 on p. 99), here there is a passionate outburst of frustrated emotion. Was there ever a more violent protestation of love than this?

Ex.100

Small wonder that one of the critics of the day attacked Berlioz for wanting to invent new rhythms, as though composers had no right to do such a thing. The orchestral players of his time must indeed have scratched their heads over this newfangled stuff. Imagine the sensation, then, at the first rehearsal when Berlioz

---

[1] His detractors would say 'because he couldn't harmonize it', but I feel this to be a narrow-minded judgement.

called for no fewer than four drummers simultaneously at the end of this movement. It is one of the greatest examples of virtuosity in orchestration and every serious student of music should examine the last twenty-five bars of this Adagio with some care. Berlioz reintroduces the cor anglais melody with which he had begun; but now, between each of its phrases, he inserts the most extraordinary effects of distant thunder, scored in such a way that at times four timpani are being played together, making chords of drums. I quote two bars to show the kind of texture he creates.

Ex. 101

No words of mine can describe the effect of this brilliantly calculated sound; in less skilful hands this coda could easily have been corny in the extreme. After all, a shepherd's pipe alternating with a few distant rumbles of thunder is not the most original of conceptions, and especially to our ears today, it savours too much of the sentimentality of a Victorian engraving. However, Berlioz handles his unusual orchestral palette with uncanny sensitivity, and the soft grumble of deep-voiced timpani is awe-inspiring in its majesty.

These same drums make a fascinating link into the next movement, a strand of colour that binds them together. This is probably fortuitous, though, since this famous 'March to the Stake' is taken from an earlier opera of Berlioz, *Les Francs-Juges*. If the scoring is preserved from the previous version it is even more remarkable, since it means that these extraordinary new sounds were conceived in his early twenties. The march begins with two timpani in G and B♭, *pizzicato* double basses divided into a four-part chord of G minor, and low grunts on horns and bassoons that seem to belong more to the pages of Stravinsky's *Firebird* than to a work written a mere three years after Beethoven's death—indeed quite possibly while Beethoven was still alive, if the scoring remains intact from the earlier version. Gradually the sound accumulates, by the addition of instruments rather than by a crescendo, as though more and more people were falling in behind the tumbril; then, after a sudden explosion of sound, 'cellos and basses declaim a curiously shaped theme based on a descending scale.

Ex. 102

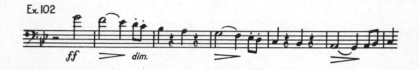

This is repeated many times with varying counterpoints, one of which is its own self in inversion, i.e. a similar scale in contrary motion. Suddenly the dark menace of the first few pages is swept away in a triumphant march scored for full wind and brass. One can only assume that Berlioz sees himself as the victim, and imagines that the mob is on his side; thus the procession to his doom becomes a path of glory. Although there is a tremendous weight of sound here Berlioz does not abuse it, and there are moments of striking contrast. One passage in particular shows an astonishing ear for colour, breaking up the scale theme quoted above into kaleidoscopic fragments.

Ex. 103

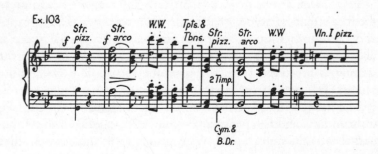

In the very next bar he builds up the sound from a wispy *p* to an electrifying *f* by again using four timpani in G, B♭, D, and F in succession. A little later on, we find the much-discussed opposition of the chords of D flat major and G minor, a harmonic conflict so unusual that the players of the time all questioned it: Berlioz obligingly puts a footnote at the bottom of the score assuring us that it is not a mistake.

Right at the end of the movement we find the most dramatic touch of all; we are to assume that our hero has now reached the scaffold. The procession halts, and for a fleeting moment we hear a single clarinet playing the motto theme—a last thought of the beloved. An immense chord cuts it off in mid-phrase, and with a dull *pizzicato* thud the dismembered head bounces into the basket. A shattering roll of drums and sixteen chords of G major finish the movement in a mood of relentless savagery. About sixty-five years later Strauss used an identical technique in *Till Eulenspiegel*; once more one is made to realize that Berlioz anticipated practically every orchestral trick of the second half of the nineteenth century. From this point of view the Finale is perhaps the most remarkable movement of all, as we shall now see.

In the Witches' Sabbath we find spectacular orchestral invention and bad music in roughly equal proportions; it is worth remembering that Moussorgsky's *Night on a Bare Mountain* with which this movement could most easily be compared was written thirty-seven years later. *The Sorcerer's Apprentice* of Dukas with which it also has some points of resemblance was even further away —sixty-seven years. There was literally nothing even remotely like this to have influenced Berlioz; in the portrayal of the macabre and the supernatural he started from scratch, and for all its faults as a composition, this movement must remain a *tour de force* of orchestral colouring. The whole symphony could be called the *Rite of Spring* of the nineteenth century.

The finale begins with a high shimmer of violins and violas, divided into eight parts, with savage growls in 'cellos and double basses, reinforced by a pair of timpani. Spiky semiquavers drift

down like dead leaves or a spatter of raindrops, and then 'cellos
and basses have an extraordinary bar of ominous rumbling in
which they are both divided, while sharp-edged strings pluck out
a fanfare above. Distant horn-calls, bat-like screeches—all the
romantic trappings of Thomas Lovell Beddoes are to be found
here. The literary world was suddenly fascinated by phantas-
magoria. Edgar Allan Poe was just beginning to write, and nine
years before the *Symphonie Fantastique*, the youthful Beddoes had
written a perfect anticipation of its mood:

> . . . It was dark and cold;
> A putrid steam rose from the clammy mould;
> The moon darts through a crevice: at his lips
> He sees a scull's mouth yawn, which thickly drips
> With nauseous moisture; upward to his thigh
> He stood in bones and dust of bodies dead;
> And part was newly melting, part was dry,
> And part, with recent slaughter, glaring red.[1]

Curiously enough, Berlioz describes a scene not unlike this in
his memoirs, when, in his early days as a medical student, he was
taken to a positive charnel-house of a dissecting room. Its effect
on his highly sensitive mind can be imagined.

It is in such a macabre setting then that we now discover the
motto theme once more; but no longer does it sustain the mood
of aloof beauty which had distinguished it in the second and third
movements. Shrill and grotesque on the high E flat clarinet, the
theme cavorts like the third witch in *Macbeth*.

Ex. 104
Allegro

etc.

---

[1] Thomas Lovell Beddoes: *The Improvisatore*: stanza XXIII.

Soon this version is taken up by the whole pack of woodwind; strings and brass add to the tumult. Suddenly the music climbs down to an almost inaudible low C; in a tense hush, near to silence, we hear the distant clang of two bells. There is a flicker of reaction in the waiting throng, instantly quelled by an abrupt and commanding gesture. Again the bells ring out, again there is a similar reaction. The scene is painted so vividly that one can visualize every detail. The ritual begins, as two tubas and four bassoons in unison chant the *Dies Irae*, a traditional melody dating back to medieval times.

Ex.105

With what appears to be complete independence the two bells continue to chime at irregular intervals while the *Dies Irae* theme is diminished, first into dotted crochets and then into a hopping 6/8 rhythm:

Ex.106

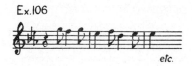

The bleak angularity of some of the scoring here conveys a unique quality of sound, and its 'modernity' is remarkable. It seems a pity that Berlioz is suddenly seized with academic aspirations and launches forth into a fugue, of all things. He justifies it by describing it as the 'Witches' Round Dance', and indeed one can imagine them joining in group by group. The slight impression of a sort of Sir Roger de Coverley's Coven is dispelled by a series of jagged Amens that cut across the dance in a positively jazz-like rhythm:

These chords are taken up with increasing enthusiasm till they pervade practically the whole orchestra. As in the first movement, the listener gains a tremendous impression of pace, a word that I use as distinct from tempo. The *Dies Irae* theme returns as the music dies down to a low grumble, then a further crescendo leads to what Berlioz obviously regarded as the climax of the symphony. In tones of Jack Hornerish pride he indicates on the score that the *Dies Irae* and the Witches Round Dance are here combined; and indeed they are married with little difficulty. As a feat of composition it is scarcely in the same category as the finale of the 'Jupiter' Symphony, but to a composer as insecure in technique as Berlioz it must have seemed a joyful discovery. As soon as he can forget about such academic props the flame of genius flares up again, and he produces some electrifying sounds. Especially worth mentioning is the extraordinary gasping effect he achieves by dynamics as eccentric as these:

$$|\text{♩. ♩.} |\text{♩. ♩.} |\text{♩. ♩.} | \textit{etc. simile}$$
$$p\mathord{<}\mathit{ff}\mathord{>}pp\mathord{<}\mathit{ff}\mathord{>}pp\mathord{<}\mathit{ff}\mathord{>}$$

The end is calculated to leave the listener exhausted, reeling beneath the impact of the relatively huge resources which Berlioz here deploys with such fabulous skill. Were this work to have been written after 1870 it would be justifiable to belittle it on the grounds of its periodical ineptness and occasional miscalculations. History is not to be denied, however, and the inescapable fact remains that in orchestral virtuosity and exploration of tone and rhythm this symphony leapt so far into the future that one can be

indulgent if it loses its footing in places. Its psychological significance is probably equally as great, for with this work, music
plunged headlong into the giddy current of Romanticism; the
intrusion of the composer's Ego in so blatantly autobiographical
a manner was a milestone; it remained for composers of a later
period to unleash the Id.

CHAPTER VII

BRAHMS

Symphony No. 2 in D, Op. 73 (1877)

1. Allegro non troppo. 2. Adagio non troppo. 3. Allegretto grazioso (Quasi Andantino) alternating with Presto ma non assai. 4. Allegro con spirito.

Orchestra: 2 flutes; 2 oboes; 2 clarinets; 2 bassoons; 4 horns; 2 trumpets; 3 trombones; 1 tuba; 1 timpanist; normal complement of strings.

Brahms composed this symphony in the summer of 1877 while staying at Pörtschach, on the Wörthersee. It appears to have caused him little difficulty since it was finished in a matter of months—a striking contrast to the First Symphony, over which he had laboured for fifteen years. The first performance was given on 30 December of the same year in Vienna, with Hans Richter conducting. The work was rapturously received by the Viennese audience, but had a rather chilly reception some ten days later when Brahms himself directed a performance in Leipzig.

I T IS CURIOUS that a composer who is now acknowledged as one of the great masters of form should have been so unsure of himself when it came to writing a symphony. Whether Brahms was really as overawed by the stature of Beethoven as he made out, or whether he felt that the symphony as a form was in a state of decline it is impossible to say. The indisputable fact remains that his first symphony did not appear until he was forty-three years old, and its opus number (68) is clear enough indication of how much music he already had behind him at the time. Once he had tasted success with his initial venture he was quick to follow it up, so much so that his four symphonies were all written within a span of nine years.

In comparison with the sombre, tragic mood of the First Symphony, the Second is an astonishing contrast—lyrical, sunny, and full of a quality of serenity which at times warms to a positive radiance. It is as though Brahms were heaving a gigantic sigh of relief at having overcome the immense obstacle which his First Symphony seems to have represented. To dismiss the D major symphony as a mere divertimento, as some writers have tended to do, is, however, a gross underestimate of its value; the nineteenth-century Leipzig critic who complained about its 'prettiness', claiming that he expected more weighty things from a composer of Brahms's quality, failed to realize that here was a work of truly dazzling craftsmanship, in which Brahms displays a fertility of technical resource which is unfailing in its inventiveness. Of the four, this is the most rewarding symphony to study, not because it says anything more profound than the others, but because in it we can most clearly see the hand of a supreme craftsman at work. We cannot expect to acquire the attributes of genius, however hard we study; what we can do is to see how genius is channelled and directed by technique.

The very first page of the score is as rich a source of material as you will find anywhere. On the face of it, it is simply a disarming melody:

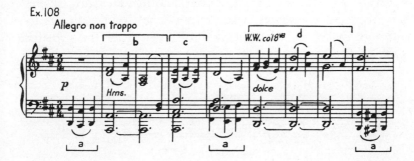

Nothing could be more deceptive; the ear may connect all this up into a continuous strand, but to Brahms it is a series of fragments, each one of which is as potentially fruitful as an acorn.

Thus in the first bar, which also appears in the bass of bars 5 and 9, we find the three-note motive (*a*) from which any number of developments will be seen to grow; in the first seventy bars alone this little pattern appears over thirty times in one form or other. Bars 2 and 3 must be considered as another detachable unit (*b*); bar 4 is yet another (*c*). (The fact that it is also an inversion of bar 1 is, I think, no more than a coincidence.) Lastly, the four-bar woodwind phrase (*d*), though more complete in itself than the mere snippets we have detached so far, is equally liable to be chopped out of its context and developed as a separate entity.

For the moment horns and woodwind continue on an untroubled course; the violins bide their time in patience. When they do come in, they have a bare suggestion of the bar 1 figure, both elongated and extended.

This descending chain seems to dissolve as it dies down to a single muttered drum-roll; trombones brood quietly while the woodwind periodically remind us of bar 1 again. Then, in the forty-fourth bar, the sun comes out, and these tentative suggestions of melody flower at last into a lyrical outburst from the strings. Even here, though, the three-note pattern from the first bar is of prime importance.

This new theme overlaps itself very neatly, and Brahms makes a positive daisy-chain out of it, instrument after instrument coming in impetuously, each without allowing its predecessor to finish.

The music grows bolder and more severe; soon we find the three-note pattern striding firmly across the score; matched against it are these choppy quavers:

Ex.III

It only takes a little thought to realize that this aggressive new counter-subject, which I have called *b2*, is none other than a contraction of the opening horn theme (*b*) from the second and third bar of the work (see Ex. 108). As the tension increases, the three-note pattern (*a*) gets squashed up, until its condensed version suddenly breaks right across the pseudo-heroic mood of the music and beguiles us with the most enchanting musical chuckles.

Ex. II2

The music seems about to disintegrate as Brahms reduces it to a scatter of brief chords and snatches of the *b2* phrase; then he seems to take a grip on himself in a patch of glorious sustained harmony, and at last the true second subject appears.

Ex. II3

Here the 'cellos steal the violas' glory by taking the upper line; above, the two violin parts interchange decorative fragments which are all based on *b2*. In such a way does Brahms relate these new events with the very beginning of the work. For some thirty bars, he now allows this new theme to have its head; as it grows in assurance it gradually dispenses with its links with the past. The references to the *b2* motive vanish, and wind and strings take turns in extending this gracious second subject. Suddenly a violent new rhythm breaks the spell. Jagged, leaping octaves, harsh syncopations, rough dissonances explode into a tempestuous new version of bar 1.

The rhythm is made even more agitated by tying over the last of each group to the first of the next,

etc. For several pages of the score this savage pattern persists; around it surge uneasy memories of the first three notes of section *d* (Ex. 108)—reappearing for the first time. After a tremendous climax the second subject comes in again, somewhat shaken; an almost feverish counterpoint on a flute harps incessantly on the two adjacent notes of *a* until, exhausted, the music sinks back to an uneasy rest. At this point Brahms demands the classic repeat of the exposition, but in this symphony conductors usually disregard his instructions.

Until now, the composer has mainly occupied himself with the first three bars of the symphony. This may seem a somewhat startling assertion, but apart from the second subject, which as I have shown is cleverly integrated with the horn-call (*b*) from bars 2 and 3, practically everything that we have heard so far has been closely related to those first 'germs' *a* and *b* of Ex. 108. It is interesting now to see how Brahms transfers his interests to *c* and *d* when he comes to the development.

The first inkling that we are moving in a new direction comes with a sudden switch to F major—a fairly positive denial of the 'home' key of D, since it cancels out both F♯ and C♯, the two salient accidentals of D major. The horn reminds us of the opening phrases.

As you can see, the oboe at once seizes on the fragment labelled *c* and extends it into a sequence. This is the cue for a general increase in severity; the meltingly lyrical quality of the music is replaced by something much more 'academic', as though Brahms were addressing himself to some imagined critic—after all, this *is* a symphony. The other wind instruments take up the oboe's extension of *c* more strongly; the 'cellos and basses match them stride for stride. Before we realize it we are pitched headlong on to a fugal sea; at last bars 6–9 of the first page come into their own (see Ex. 108), and the neglected phrase (*d*) reigns triumphant.

Even here one marvels at the way Brahms keeps an ever-watchful eye on his material. Many patterns of quavers would fit against a main subject of this calibre, but he chooses one which is still related to what has gone before. The descending pattern (*c*) which had been established by the oboe in the passage quoted in Ex. 115 is tightened up into a brittle counter-subject.

becomes

The struggle continues. Any suspicions we may have had that Brahms was just coasting along writing a sort of glorified serenade must be dispelled by the sense of intellectual grappling which we now experience. At its height, the trombones (which are used with the most masterly economy in this score) suddenly cut into the texture with grinding dissonances that put the bar 1 motive on the rack.

Over and over again these jagged outlines spill through the score—shortened, lengthened, tumbling one over the other, rocks spewed out with volcanic force. In time *a* and *b* are actually combined, as the wind and brass hammer out the first two notes of *b* while the strings hack their way through *a*.

Ex. 120

Even the serene melody quoted in Ex. 110 is forced into the minor key by the overall mood of agitation. At last the supreme climax of the movement is reached; the whole orchestra reiterates over and over again the pairs of notes indicated as *b* in the example above. After eight bars of *ff* there is a sudden drop in the tension; horns and trumpets continue quietly with fragments of *b*, but the strings remember once more the slowest version of *a*,

Ex. 121

A last convulsive chord leads to a slow descent in the woodwind which brings us back to the recapitulation. The combination of themes here is so masterly that I make no apology for quoting a few bars in short score. There could be no more graphic proof of the concentration that a real master brings to his task. Composition consists far more of rejection than acceptance; anything irrelevant is pushed aside by the composer; everything possible is done to relate theme to theme, pattern to pattern.

Ex. 122

The recapitulation follows a roughly similar course to the first few pages of the exposition; in detail, however, it is infinitely richer. What was before a bare sketch is now filled in with intricate counter-melodies, warmer harmony, richer scoring. By chopping out a whole section of some thirty bars, Brahms brings in the second subject much earlier than before, and, since the point has now been made, he no longer bothers to underline its relationship to the first subject. Once again, though, we must realize the danger of sitting back as passive listeners; the recapitulation is not an empty formula, for Brahms has many new pleasures in store for us. In particular we want to look out when the first horn begins to rhapsodize on this version of *c*.

Ex. 123

From now on, this horn part reaches out further and further until, in a typical Brahmsian sunset, the music dies down to a slower tempo. In a soft haze the violins muse over *b* while the 'cellos and basses extend *a*. With the utmost delicacy the woodwind recall the little chuckling phrase from Ex. 112. All is gentleness and peace, and the movement ends as it had begun, with a tender simplicity that is far from naïve. It seems more as if Brahms had fallen in love with the material of the movement; this affectionate farewell shows his reluctance to part with it.

It is essential to hear a movement like this many times before you can really claim familiarity with it. There is so much detail packed into every page of the score that only close analysis will reveal all its secrets. Such craftsmanship is not merely an incidental facet of the music; it is an integral part of its greatness. If we just sit back and say that this section is pretty, that one is loud, this part is getting slower, or even 'turn the volume down a bit, dear, I'm reading', we are (by our intellectual indifference) reducing the music to the level of any orchestral background noise. Brahms must have exerted every ounce of his mental energy when writing this, and it is our duty to make a corresponding effort to get to the heart of every marvellously constructed phrase. Music is not just an emotional stimulus—a pattern of sedatives and shocks; it is something far more significant. Listen intelligently and with understanding and you cannot fail to feel an intense gratitude that any one man had the vision, the humanity, the intellect, and the craftsmanship that go to make up such a masterpiece.

Of the four movements in this symphony, the second is the most difficult to grasp. One is soon aware of its gravity, of its determination to avoid the type of sentimentality that we find in the long horn solo in Tchaikovsky's Fifth Symphony; but analysis is of little help. What is needed most is simply a willingness to soak oneself in its beauty, to respond to the mood Brahms clearly has in mind. Much of the movement is concerned with shapes rather than melodies—in fact, one of the most important features could be represented diagrammatically by two lines approaching each other.

This contrary motion is of the greatest importance, since it imposes a certain mathematical quality of detachment, of abstraction on otherwise emotional material.

Ex. 124

Brahms seems determined to keep any unduly obvious sentimentality at bay, and much of this movement is fugal in style. Do
not be misled, though, into classifying as new those themes which
are actually old ones disguised. For example, half-way through
the opening melody, which is coloured in the rich yet sombre
hue that only the 'cellos can give, we find this phrase:

Ex.125

Brahms needs only four notes out of this to build a whole new
section, a section which at first glance would appear to be a
completely new development. The horn leads off with this curious
rocking theme:

Ex.126

It is taken up in turn by oboes, flutes, and 'cellos and basses—
certainly not as a strict fugue, but at least in the spirit of one.
Where does it come from? Look at the fifth to the eighth notes
of Ex. 125 and you will see at once.

The severity of much of this movement is softened by a
delicate contrasting tune in F# major. Scored mostly for woodwind with a *pizzicato* bass giving it a suggestion of a dance-
rhythm, it is notable for the gentle syncopations which Brahms
may well have learnt from Schumann. The sunnier mood which
this tune induces does not last for long, and soon the strings
present yet another theme, again of an intensely serious kind. The
unity of this movement is remarkable; we have seen how one
small segment of the opening melody can be the mainspring of a
whole new section. Brahms now accomplishes this same conjuring
trick once more. Take the last few notes of Ex. 124:

Ex. 127

Although it is quite probable that Brahms had no particular intention of echoing this pattern later in the movement, there is unquestionably a fairly close family resemblance between it and the new serious theme which the strings first present in bar 45. I will transpose it down so that the similarity of contour can be appreciated more easily.

Ex. 128

Compare this in turn with the horn theme in Ex. 126, and the feeling of what one might call a musical blood-tie becomes even more striking.

This new theme goes through a somewhat stormy episode in which Brahms makes much use of the three rising quavers with which it begins. There is also a fascinating ghost, an ominous three-note phrase, B♭ A B♭ or E F♮ E, which could conceivably be a memory of bar 1 of the first movement. If the music were by César Franck I would unhesitatingly assert that this was a deliberate back-reference; since it is by Brahms, I tend to feel that it is probably a subconscious echo and no more.[1] It is important in so far as it leads us back to the initial theme whose ultimate unwinding is marked by various decorations and perturbations before it finally sinks to an uneasy rest.

The third movement was an instant success, having to be repeated at many of the earlier performances of the symphony. The mature Brahms seems to have wanted to slow down the hectic scherzo which Beethoven had perfected. Many of his chamber works show a preference for an easygoing amble rather

[1] For a further discussion of this type of 'quotation', see p. 122.

than a breathless gallop, and this movement remains in the memory as a gentle Allegretto even although 142 of its 240 bars are marked 'presto ma non assai'. In form, it is a combination of three things: a rondo, a set of variations, and an inversion of the classical Scherzo and Trio. At first glance it seems to be A B A C A, which would make it a rondo. We then realize that B is a variation of A, and that C is another variation; this puts it into the second category. Lastly we remember that it is the third movement of a symphony and consequently that it stems from the scherzo and trio of classical usage; but whereas the trio was traditionally taken at an easier tempo than the scherzo, here Brahms introduces what I have termed an inversion of the form by substituting slow-quick-slow-quick-slow for the more conventional quick-slow-quick-slow-quick.[1] All of which is merely intended to show that there is more originality to this than its attractive presence would suggest.

It begins with an enchanting theme on the oboe.

Ex.129

Meanwhile, the 'cellos are busy pretending to be guitars, their softly plucked accompaniment only emphasizing the serenade-like character of the tune. The upper strings stay aloof from the proceedings for thirty-two bars. When they do come in the mood is broken, and with a lightness that almost suggests Mendelssohn they lift the oboe-tune into more airy spheres.

Ex.130

[1] For a similar example in his chamber music, cf. the second movement of the Violin Sonata in A major, Op. 100.

The 'Midsummer Night's Dream' atmosphere is heightened by a sudden burst of rowdiness, as though Bottom and his troupe had blundered into some fairy glade.

Ex.131

Ex.131a (later)

Even this will be seen to be an inversion of the opening theme, albeit a fairly free one. The bustle continues until a few more measured beats from the 'cellos lead us back to the original tempo. This is a moment of pure magic, for Brahms now harmonizes the oboe tune in a subtly different way, changing one's whole conception of its emotional intensity. Its initial purity is replaced by a haunting pathos; daylight gives way to dusk. Compare these two phrases and you will see what I mean.

Ex.132   Ex.132a

The tune takes a somewhat different direction now, seeming to become a little more serious with implications of E minor creeping in. In particular, Brahms keeps stressing the little triplet figure from the fourth bar, whose importance we only realize fully when the next Presto section begins. It proves to be the very mainspring of the new tempo as the strings lead the way into a second dance. Equally Mendelssohnian in character, it employs the simplified version, as in Ex. 131a. In time, this is stripped down to a bare skeleton before the gracious opening tune makes its final appearance. As a coda, we find a last romantic paroxysm from the strings—a phrase which seems so akin to the slow movement of Mozart's Piano Concerto in A major (K.488) that one can only assume a subconscious memory on Brahms's part.

Ex.133

Mozart's rhythm

Such unconscious imitations are not important—Brahms himself said that plagiarism was one of the silliest topics of stupid people —but they are interesting in that they emphasize the almost universally felt emotional patterns that seem to go with certain intervals and harmonies. It is as though composers of different ages and different nationalities were able to draw upon some common store of experience, a store from which a group of notes is indelibly stamped with melancholy, brilliance, tenderness, or pathos, according to its contour.[1]

The finale is a magnificent and complex movement in sonata form. In common with the other movements, it shows Brahms to be much occupied with dissection. We have seen how in the opening Allegro he abstracted small fragments of the first melody and developed them as separate units. Here we find the same technique being employed. He begins with a quiet and mysterious theme, of which the second bar is particularly important in that it frequently becomes a reiterated bass, or *ostinato*, to use the proper term.

Ex.134

etc.

We must be prepared for bar 1 to be compressed into four equal quavers:

Ex.135

[1] See Deryck Cooke's most interesting study *The Language of Music* (Oxford University Press, 1959).

Bar 2 we already know is destined to become a bass-line—in fact, the 'cellos and basses are immediately hypnotized by it and go on playing it a further four times while the violins climb up to the high D. Bars 5 and 6 show falling fourths coupled in pairs; these too bear a suggestion of things to come, for from them springs this important if subsidiary theme:

Ex.136

All this is presented with bated breath and an air of mystery that is intriguing to say the least; suddenly this mood is swept aside, and a riotous full orchestra takes up the theme as if to say, 'Why, there you were all the time!' A down-to-earth *tutti*[1] blows all thoughts of fantasy from our heads. The falling fourths are broken up into abrupt little phrases— ♪♪♩ ; ♪♪♩ ; and much is made of the compressed version of bar 1. There seems no reason to stop the general rejoicing until, with a dramatic gesture that reduces the rest of the orchestra to a sudden hushed *piano*, a single high clarinet introduces a new sustained theme that changes the whole atmosphere. Only a subdued murmur of Ex. 135 in the strings keeps this new idea 'in the family'. A few wide-spaced harmonies on the woodwind lead us to the second subject.

Ex. 137

Just as the second subject of the first movement was subtly related to the opening bars (see Ex. 113), so here Brahms unifies the finale by presenting constant reminders of Ex. 135 against this lyrical new theme. At first we assume that this is no more than a characteristic display of craftsmanship, but with the imaginative skill that distinguishes all truly great composers, Brahms seizes on

[1] *tutti* = a passage for full orchestra; a term especially used in concerto-form.

this decorative fragment and develops it in the grand manner. The range of the phrase is widened until it gains a positively heroic stature.

On the face of it this seems a far cry from Ex. 134, but it is a legitimate extension of the first bar of the finale, and must be appreciated as such. The running scales at the end of Ex. 138 are passed around the woodwind section with some enthusiasm before a curious rhythm with a Scotch snap to it rounds off the exposition.

The development is a good deal more involved than is usual in a symphonic finale. After a brief reminder of the first four bars of Ex. 134, the music seems to disintegrate into brief phrases which appear to be leading nowhere. In fact, they are leading to the obscure world of F♯ minor, a wonderland which causes the opening theme to stand on its head.

As will be seen from a closer look at this, the phrases in quavers with a bracket below them are a quickened inversion of the crochet phrases with a bracket above. Brahms plays turn and turn-about with these two fragments until a sudden rather cross entry of Ex. 136 (now in the minor) chases them away. With increasing intensity, and propelled by strong syncopations, the music builds to a passionate climax. Most unexpectedly this leads not to a triumphant restatement of the opening material but to one of the most intimate and magical moments of the entire symphony. In the warm radiance of F♯ major we suddenly find a gently rocking motive that opens a whole new world of emotion.

What a wonderfully subtle variation of Ex. 134 this is, as the rhythmic pattern below reveals. Intermingled with this touching development we find sundry echoes of Ex. 136, but for the most part they are now in the minor. With an effect of distant majesty, like a great mountain seen far off, the trombones enunciate the first bell-like notes of Ex. 136 in minims; a slow *tremolando* in the violins enhances the impression of distance. It is the dawn of a new day, for in a moment Brahms leads us back to the recapitulation.

This behaves in an orthodox manner, taking a shortened route to the second subject which duly appears in the tonic key of D major. The various developments that we have experienced are passed in review, until in a last blaze of triumph the trumpets and horns lift the second subject from its normal contemplative self to a mood of heroic rejoicing. Whenever Brahms felt particularly pleased with a work he would joke about it in terms that were the exact opposite to the truth. For instance, of the great Scherzo of the B♭ Piano Concerto he said that it was 'a tiny wisp of a scherzo'. Of this symphony he wrote that it was so mournful that the score would have to be printed on black-edged paper. To those who knew him, such a remark indicated the special delight that comes with the knowledge of a job well done.

CHAPTER VIII

SIBELIUS

Symphony No. 2 in D, Op. 43 (1901)

1. Allegretto—poco allegro. 2. Tempo andante, ma rubato—allegro—andante sostenuto. 3. Vivacissimo—lento e soave—tempo primo. 4. Allegro moderato.

Orchestra: 2 flutes; 2 oboes; 2 clarinets; 2 bassoons; 4 horns; 3 trumpets; 3 trombones; 1 tuba; 1 timpanist; normal complement of strings.

This symphony was written in 1901, two years after the First Symphony, at a time when the composer was thirty-six years old. First performance on 8 March 1902 at a concert devoted entirely to his works. For several years around this period Sibelius was greatly worried by ear-trouble, and no doubt fears of deafness afflicted him and caused him a severe emotional crisis. Despite this, the general impression we gain from this symphony is one of optimism, an optimism which perhaps reflects the Italian spring, since it was mainly written in the hilly country behind Rapallo, where Sibelius had rented a small work-room.

I T IS IRONIC that whereas the inclusion of a Sibelius symphony in such a book as this would have been regarded as inevitable in the nineteen-thirties, today one must almost adopt a defensive attitude to justify his inclusion. For some reason or another Sibelius has become a rather 'unfashionable' composer, even though many sincere and knowledgeable musicians believe him to be truly great. I think the principal reason for this is simply that the best way to be looked on as unfashionable is to scorn fashion, and if ever a composer did that it was Sibelius. At a time when experiments in every aspect of music were rife he stuck firmly to his own somewhat traditional style. While the First Symphony shows evidence of many influences—Tchaikovsky, Rimsky-Korsakov, and Grieg are perhaps the most noticeable—once he entered his own particular world, a world which he first saw clearly in this Second Symphony, he continued on his own way. The post-Wagnerian melting-pot, in which every imaginable form of musical experiment was tried, applauded, rejected, and resurrected, affected him not at all. In enviable isolation he went on writing what he wanted to, untouched by the emotional or intellectual excesses that were changing the face of European music. His compositions range from the supremely concentrated distillation of the Fourth Symphony to the unabashed popularity of the *Valse Triste*.[1] On occasion he will despise melody, concentrating all his resources on tiny fragments of a mere three or four notes; in more expansive mood, he can write a long, sustained tune that for sheer melodic beauty knows few parallels. There cannot be many themes as beautiful and yet as intensely personal as that in the slow movement of the violin concerto, in which the rich tones of the solo violin are enshrouded in the romantic gloom of horns and bassoons while the ghostly footsteps of the plucked strings pad furtively through the dusk. Yet although the atmosphere of this movement positively reeks of nineteenth-century Romanticism, Sibelius manages to present its Byronic fantasies in a completely new light. Where a Liszt or a Wagner would have become obsessed with a literary image, and where they would have allowed the musical form to be overshadowed by a picture, a story, or some figment of a non-musical imagination, he keeps the movement under iron control. The sensuous passion may be there, but it is kept in heroic restraint. He is a true classicist; his works are the product of a marvellously ordered mind, and while such control in lesser hands might lead to mere worthiness, in his case it leads to true worth.

The strong classical bent we find in him inevitably drew him towards the symphony as a form, even although it had lost its

---

[1] Those who accuse Sibelius of commercialism in writing the *Valse Triste* should remember that he sold it outright to his publisher for £5, thereby forfeiting any further royalty.

appeal for most other composers. The reason for this mass deser-
tion of a form ennobled by Mozart and Haydn, Beethoven and
Brahms is fairly clear. As I have constantly stressed, tonality or a
sense of key is the basis on which the symphony had been built.
Once the tonal freedom of Wagner had loosened the ties of key
the whole foundation of the symphony was weakened; modulation
ceases to register in music which is in a constant state of tonal flux,
and without significant modulation the architectural implications
of a large-scale movement are changed almost beyond recognition. In the first years of the twentieth century, other composers
were striking out in all kinds of new directions—the impression-
ism of the French, the Russian folk-art of Stravinsky, the neurotic
(and erotic) symbolism of the atonal composers such as Schönberg
and Berg. On all this experimentalism Sibelius turned his back,
choosing to tunnel deeper into the heart of the greatest classical
form.

Like all the major classical composers, he prefers to work with
fragments rather than melodies. It is a basic property of music that
all sounds breed a certain emotion; this group of notes[1] bespeaks
loneliness, another conveys brilliance, another gaiety, and so on.
The problem for the composer, then, is that he is wrestling intel-
lectually with material which is in its very nature emotional.
There is little enough emotional significance in a phrase like

Ex. 141

which is what makes it good symphonic material; there may be
intensity in the *playing*, in the sheer sound of the orchestra, but
the phrase itself is pretty well negative. If a composer writes a tune,
as he does in a slow movement, the tune becomes the master. It
dictates the emotion, and even its creator must follow it, supporting it with suitable harmonies and embroidering it with decorations of one kind or the other. In his First Symphony, Sibelius fell

[1] Even a single chord—a 'bare' fifth, a 'rich' major triad, an 'anguished' ninth.

into this trap, choosing themes that were too positive in their emotional content, and which consequently proved intractable in development. In all the later symphonies he uses much more neutral material—fragments which he presents to us as disconnected, apparently irreconcilable units, and which he then forges before our very eyes into a marvellous cohesion.

Although I have emphasized the conservative nature of Sibelius's genius, it is a fallacy to imagine that his symphonies in any way resemble those of Beethoven or Brahms. His ideas of form are entirely different from those of his predecessors. It is difficult to find an exact simile to elucidate the differences, but even a comparison with something mechanical will help. Suppose that we compare the first movement of a symphony to a watch. In the classical symphony the composer showed you the watch complete in the first section or exposition. 'Look at this watch,' he would say. 'This is one side of it, the first side, and here is the other side, the second; and they are joined together by the bit in the middle.'[1] In the development section he would take the watch to pieces, concentrate on one (or several) of its component parts, or build new patterns from its works. In the third part, the recapitulation, he reassembles the watch in the light of experience gained and gives you the satisfaction of a second look at the completed article —at which point you can lean back feeling that you now know a lot more about watches.

Sibelius has a technique which is almost exactly opposite to this. He starts his symphony by showing you a lot of oddly shaped little bits lying about all over the score; in the development section he puts them together, allowing them to grow and co-ordinate so that you see a watch being built; finally, as likely as not, he takes them all apart again, leaving you with the scattered pieces and a sense of 'Would you believe it? Those different little bits were related to each other all the time.' Naturally, this is something of a simplification, but it should be enough to make Sibelius's individuality as a musical craftsman evident. While it could be argued that Brahms also offers us a number of fragments at the

---

[1] First subject—bridge passage—second subject.

start of his Second Symphony (see Ex. 108), they at least *sound* like one melody; the essential difference between his technique and that of Sibelius is that the later composer presents his ideas as disconnected gobbets, often divided one from the other by silences. In fact, there is one great historical precedent for the Sibelian concept of form, and that is the B minor Sonata of Liszt. This astonishing work anticipates almost exactly the structural innovations with which Sibelius is normally credited.

The Second Symphony begins with a figure which sounds like an accompaniment but which is actually vitally important.

Ex. 142

On top of this unassuming opening gambit a perky little wood-wind theme appears, like a distant fanfare.

Ex. 143

The last few notes of this are underlined by the horns, who softly repeat them at a somewhat slower tempo. As if to empha-size the importance of this material still more, Sibelius repeats it a couple more times, albeit with slight modifications of pitch. On each occasion the change of rhythm in the horns gives a curious feeling of uncertainty, as though the composer were still not convinced of the worth of this material. Finally, the music dissolves into a longish silence. Two flutes make a tentative sugges-tion which seems ineffective; bassoons echo it half-heartedly and then launch themselves into a fanfare-like motive which one feels has been stolen from the rightful preserve of the trumpets.

Ex.144

The hollow laughter of the flutes' trill mocks the bassoons into silence, and then, totally unsupported by harmony, the violins suddenly project a long melodic line. Even Berlioz never presented a theme as baldly as this.

Ex.145

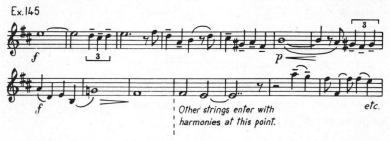

Other strings enter with harmonies at this point.   etc.

Classical training might lead us to think (quite wrongly) that this is a second subject, but all in all the whole symphony up to this point would seem to be an extraordinary hotchpotch of disconnected ideas. Any attempt to relate them one to another is sheer folly, for Sibelius intends them to be disconnected. Here, laid out for us to see, are the wheels, the springs, the hands of his watch—little snatches of tunes, harmonies, rhythms from which he will ultimately build a whole movement. To add further to the confusion there are curious vacillations of mood from tenderness to savagery.

The first truly forward impulse of the movement is heralded by a fascinating passage for *pizzicato* strings. A quickening of the tempo leads to the most significant and characteristic theme of all.

Ex.146

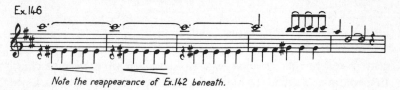

Note the reappearance of Ex.142 beneath.

Sibelius seems greatly drawn towards themes which begin with an immensely long note whose tension is dispelled by a sudden convulsion of quicker notes. This particular example generates tremendous energy; the strings begin to whirr with the precision of machinery, while abrupt little phrases on the woodwind cut sharply through the texture. Gradually the calming influence of Ex. 142 makes itself felt. A single oboe reminds us of Ex. 146, only to be answered by a bassoon which drags up a somewhat murky phrase of considerable importance.

Ex.147

The quiet dynamo hum of the strings continues while over and over again different woodwind instruments reiterate a brief angular phrase in descending fifths.

Ex.148

(sometimes only five notes)

Above all one gains an impression of tremendous drive and pace, a feeling that is only slightly eased when the music settles down on a constantly repeated G sharp on a solo kettle-drum. From this point an extensive development of Ex. 143 begins. Its treatment involves translation into a minor key, inversion, and an ingenious condensation:

Ex.149

(bar I. inverted)

The next stage is more impassioned as the strings vary this pattern still further, goaded by waspish trills from the woodwind. In a continuous ascent to higher levels they at last arrive on a high

B flat, whereupon Ex. 146 appears once more in triumph, while double basses and drums pound out the rhythm with which the symphony had so unemotionally begun. The most dramatic climax of the movement is heralded by a fanfare in which the trumpets and horns at last take over the theme the bassoons had presented so unconvincingly in the early stages (Ex. 144). As is often the case in Sibelius's music, one has the impression of immense natural forces at work as crashing brass chords cleave their way through a haze of trills on the strings.

Suddenly we find ourselves back with the familiar material of Ex. 143, although this time it is deprived of its original support (Ex. 142). Instead, the violins reveal that the last two bars of Ex. 145 can be integrated with Ex. 143. The material is presented once more in what passes for a brief recapitulation, but everything now seems infinitely *closer* than it was before. The quiet ending deliberately leaves us in the air.

The slow movement is perhaps the toughest part of the whole symphony, tough in its intent and the most taxing for the listener. There is very little truly lyrical writing in it, and it is periodically convulsed with violent primeval struggles, as though some mighty glacier were breaking up. It begins with a long drawn-out and seemingly tireless *pizzicato* for the 'cellos and double basses. The Finns are great long-distance runners, and this opening always makes me think of the numb automaton-like feeling of the weary legs of a runner plodding on and on, till at last from his tired mind there emerges a sad dark song.

The short square-cut phrases of this folk-like melody are entirely characteristic of Sibelius, as is the gradual increase of tempo that now ensues. The upper strings begin to take an interest in the proceedings until they become positively obsessed with this concentrated and savage little figure.

It is with some surprise that we realize that so ferocious a pattern can be softened to this:

This brief interlude of tenderness comes after a terrifying outburst on the full brass—one of the most electrifying moments in the whole symphony. A few bars of almost pastoral music with rippling thirds on flutes and bassoons are still not potent enough to dispel the prevailing thunderclouds. Within a relatively short time the threatening mood returns and the lower strings savagely worry at the bracketed portion of Ex. 152.

This movement is extremely long and dramatic; even in the light of the composer's subsequent achievements it must remain a landmark, for never before had the slow movement of a symphony expressed so graphically the forbidding grandeur of Nature at its most awe-inspiring. Despite its great economy of material, it gives an impression of free composition—an improvisation on the orchestra. Inevitably it will conjure up pictures in the listener's mind, of mountain crags, of dark forests, even of demons. It is, however, not a tone-poem but a symphonic movement, showing a masterly discipline in its handling of immensely striking thematic material.

I have already mentioned in the prefatory note to this analysis that the general impression we gain from this symphony is one of optimism. Although this opinion is fairly universal it is hard to substantiate in detail. It reflects three memorable impressions—the simple gaiety of the opening, the luscious oboe tune in the Scherzo, and the heroically striding theme that begins the finale. Far the greater part of the symphony is occupied with moods of agitation, severity, terror, uneasiness, and melancholy, and yet still the impression of a 'happy' score remains. Such is the potency of a key like D major. I mention this since the Scherzo is a stormy wind-blown movement of extraordinary concentration. A superficial glance at the score might lead one to imagine that the influence of his Italian surroundings had caused Sibelius to write a Tarantella.

Such a conclusion is quickly proved wrong by the ruthless savagery with which this theme is handled. Even although much of the music is *pp* it has a demoniac quality about it that suggests the winds of Hell. Driven before its perpetual gale, like a hard-pressed ship seen occasionally above the giant wave-crests, is one forlorn phrase that appears again and again in the woodwind.

For ten pages of score little else can be heard but the ceaseless drive of Ex. 153 with occasional glimpses of Ex. 154 scudding above. Suddenly there is a mysterious silence, broken only by five wide-spaced drum-beats which recede to the virtual inaudibility of *pppp*. With a magical release of tension, the famous oboe solo appears.

The nine-times repeated note with which this melody begins is of course a variation on the type of theme I have already described as a Sibelius trademark (see Ex. 146). Instead of a long held note he now gives us a pulsing repetition, but it amounts to nearly the same thing. There is something else more interesting in this tune, for once again we have an intriguing example of the way a composer's mind works. To most listeners, this melody seems unrelated to what has gone before, yet closer examination reveals this to be a false assumption. If we look at the string figuration immediately before the drum-taps, we find an exciting sequence built on this pattern:

Ex.156

Now look at the second bar of Ex. 155. What is it but an extension of this same pattern, decorated by a simple ornament? If I write it this way you will see the resemblance at once:

Ex. 157

The Scherzo is structurally simple, consisting as it does of an orthodox A B A B A pattern, with A being the *vivacissimo* section and B the lovely oboe tune. However, the final A section is not a conclusion; in fact, it would be fairer to call it C, since it consists of new material whose function it is to carry us willy-nilly into the finale. Insistent segments of rising scales push their way through the score until at last with immense pomp and majesty the great theme of the last movement unfolds. Different though it may be in character, this too is derived from the oboe melody since its first three notes are clearly the same in pattern as the first three notes of bar 2, Ex. 155.

Ex. 158

This invigorating tune is helped on its way by grinding C sharps in the bass, coupled with repeated chords in the trombones which together give an impression of some great engine throbbing. The orchestration increases in intensity until at last a typical disintegration sets in; for the first time we hear a continuously revolving phrase in quavers which Sibelius is going to use to enormous effect. It is no more than a glorified five-finger exercise but in his hands it assumes the majesty of an ocean swell. Above it, the woodwind gradually formulate a clear picture of a most important theme. To start with, we hear no more than tentative suggestions from oboe or clarinet, but at last it becomes apparent that this is more than a random counterpoint and the phrases build and combine into a great span of melody.

Ex. 159

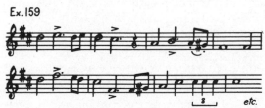

A brief sample such as this gives no idea of the extraordinary way in which Sibelius extends this pattern, spinning it out with an almost relentless quality which is enhanced still further by the constantly reiterated phrase beneath. On paper it seems a boring device; in performance it has a hypnotic power.

Such is the simplicity of the material in this movement that a detailed analysis is not at all necessary. Mention must be made of one further idea, a brief and martial phrase which recurs frequently, usually on the heavier brass.

Ex. 160

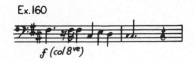

Admittedly the contour of this carries more than a suggestion of Scheherazade, but I have already mentioned the clear influence Rimsky-Korsakov seems to have had on Sibelius. The development section, if one can use such a term for a fairly loosely constructed movement, concerns itself mainly with fragments of Ex. 158 alternating with Ex. 160. It is worth remarking on the beautiful new light which is shed on Ex. 158 by playing it quietly, and with a less austere harmonization. The most memorable feature of the movement, however, is the immense accumulation of sound in the last sixteen pages of the score. Starting from a low *p*, the continuously revolving quaver pattern unfolds itself in seemingly endless repetition. For seventy bars the 'five-finger exercise' continues virtually unchanged until, with stunning effect, a cunningly placed F♯ switches the music into the major. Meantime, the sheer weight of sound has been growing until we seem engulfed in great waves of orchestral colour. It is an extension of the technique that Smetana uses in *Vltava*, but without the prettiness that tends to make the earlier work pall. There is a ruthless quality about the Sibelius that is extraordinarily impressive. Once the major has been reached, the feeling of extreme severity can be relaxed a little and a deeply satisfying re-statement of Ex. 158 brings the symphony to a triumphant conclusion. Never has emotion governed to the extent of tipping the music over into sentimentality, and the composer's iron restraint gives the whole work immense strength. Certainly in 1901 nothing was being written with greater originality than this, nor was anything more free from the all-pervading shadow of Wagner. This is great music, and it should be unaffected by the vagaries of fashion; to deny ourselves the pleasure it can bring is surely the height of folly.

CHAPTER IX

STRAVINSKY

Symphony in three movements (1945)

1. ♩= 160. 2. Andante, ♩= 76. Interlude leading to — 3. Con
moto (♩= 108)

Orchestra: 1 piccolo; 2 flutes; 2 oboes; 3 clarinets, 1 doubling bass
clarinet; 2 bassoons; 1 double bassoon; 4 horns; 3 trumpets;
3 trombones; 1 tuba; timpani; percussion; piano; harp; strings.

Notice the characteristic gesture by which Stravinsky dispenses
with any tempo indication for the first movement; he regards the
metronome mark as self-sufficient. The symphony is dedicated to
the New York Philharmonic Symphony Society and was first
performed in New York on 24 January 1946. The normal classical
orchestra has here been expanded by the use of various instruments, most of which are employed to amplify the range
available—e.g. double bassoon, bass clarinet, etc. The piano is
used almost entirely as a percussion instrument. The orchestra is
substantially reduced in size during the slow movement.

T HE CHOICE of a truly representative twentieth-century symphony poses quite a problem; I have already shown[1] that
with the collapse of tonality the foundations of the symphony as
a form were immeasurably weakened. Two courses of action are
now available to a composer wishing to perpetuate this great style
of musical architecture: either he can agree to abide by the traditional rules of tonality, which might well cause him to be dubbed
old-fashioned, or he must devise some new control which will act
as a substitute for the long-established key relationships which
have prevailed for a couple of centuries. One such substitute is the
entire new grammar and syntax of music which comes under the

[1] See p. 128.

heading of 'twelve-note composition'. Such a fundamental rejection of the known language of music did not appeal to Stravinsky,
and only in his seventies has he shown any personal leaning
towards systematic atonality—and then possibly out of a desire
not to be thought unfashionable.

The fascination about Stravinsky is that all through his life he
has delighted in giving audiences something completely different
from what they had grown to expect. Just when they had come
to understand and appreciate the rich colouring of *Firebird* and
Petrushka as an extension of nineteenth-century orchestral virtuosity, he shook the world with the primitive barbarity of *The Rite
of Spring*. Reconciled at last to that, audiences had next to grow
used to the infinitely scaled-down resources of *Les Noces*—four
pianos and percussion instead of a ninety-piece orchestra. After
all this rhythmic pounding, the dazed public was called upon to
accept a reconstitution of eighteenth-century elegance in the en-
chanted pages of *Pulcinella*. Back went Stravinsky's clock still
further, and several neo-Bach works appeared in which austere
counterpoint reigned supreme. At least the critics were now
confident that Stravinsky had finally turned his back on the highly
coloured music of his romantic Russian forebears; judge of their
confusion when he next produced *Le Baiser de la Fée*, a ballet
based on Tchaikovsky and full of rich orchestration and nineteenth-century sparkle. There seemed no limit to the caprice of
this wayward genius; and yet now, with the perspective that time
inevitably brings, we can see a fairly consistent line of development, despite occasional excursions off the track.

The basic clue to Stravinsky's approach can be summed up in
the word 'simplification'. His palate was quickly sated by the
exuberant riot of colour we find in the early ballet-scores. From
then on, he imposed ever more severe disciplines upon himself,
stripping away everything irrelevant to his purpose. The first
magnet to draw him (in *Pulcinella*) was the eighteenth century,
the Age of Reason. Then his glance went back across the centuries
to the spirit of Ancient Greece. *Oedipus Rex, Apollon Musagètes,
Persephone*, and even the *Symphony of Psalms* all share the quality

which I can best describe as being 'written in marble'. There is a feeling of classic detachment in them; the beauty of empty temples beneath hot, open skies; the sharp contrasts of dark green, white, and harsh blues; the measured movement of priests and priestesses in ancient ritual; the eternal stillness of some Homeric figure, whose sightless eyes gaze forbiddingly from the imprisoning stone.

It is paradoxical that the man who in 1913[1] must have seemed like a musical Attila, putting the traditional elements of music to the fire and the sword, should by the nineteen-twenties have become the most classically minded of all contemporary composers. Yet such is the case, and no composer since Bach more aptly illustrates one of the great truths about music—that an emotional response is more frequently an incidental (if unavoidable) by-product of it rather than a primary aim. In other words, a fugue has two sorts of beauty: the mastery with which its musical fabric is assembled, and the beauty of the actual sounds of which that fabric is composed. Of the two, the intellectual mastery is the more important. This is the very rock and foundation upon which Stravinsky's aesthetic is built. He eschews any deliberate effort to evoke emotion in an easy romantic way; for him music is a science, but also he feels it to be endowed with the dispassionate purity of a ritual. Despite the superficial appearance of complexity in his music, the most remarkable attribute of his scores is their simplicity. It is a great part of Stravinsky's genius that he is able to present the most commonplace elements of classical music in a completely new light.[2] Both the *Symphony in C* (1940) and the *Symphony in Three Movements* now to be discussed are notable for the economy with which the composer achieves effects of remarkable originality. Where other composers use materials that are intrinsically complex in themselves, Stravinsky gives us a straight common chord that is completely familiar. It is the angle of approach that is different; just as a camera can reveal new and unsuspected facets of an everyday object, so can Stravinsky uncover aspects of the chord of C major that we have never dreamed of.

[1] The year of *The Rite of Spring*.   [2] See Exx. 28 and 29, pp. 37–38.

The first movement of this symphony is strident and savage; it could be said to reflect the machine-like pulse of an industrial age. It is devoid of heart and makes only the smallest concession to emotional appeal. It is useless to seek in its brittle pages either the tenderness of Mozart, the drama of Beethoven, or the passion of Tchaikovsky. What you will find is an immensely exhilarating if somewhat ruthless drive, and a rhythmic vitality that belongs exclusively to our age. Rhythm and sonority have become the prime concern of the composer, and unless we accept this change of bias, unless we go out and meet him on his ground, we are sure to misunderstand his message.

If you were to come across this passage in a romantic piano piece it would seem perfectly orthodox.

Ex.161

Stravinsky would regard this as the tawdry trappings of Romanticism; you can't wear armour in a taxi; you'd trip over your sword getting into a bus. His technique then is to preserve the strength of such an idea but to make its presentation much starker. Instead of a sweeping tune you will find abrupt and incisive chords, cutting like machine tools into any suggestion of a soft core that the melody might have. The 'heroic' quality of Ex. 161 is stripped away and only the bare bones grimace at us.

Ex.162

The upward scale in the first bar, reinforced by a *glissando* on the piano, sounds like the ripping of a giant piece of calico. In itself this scale is important, and it is particularly worth noticing how Stravinsky uses it to break up any undue suggestion of symmetry. After an immensely striking first paragraph, the texture is suddenly reduced to a quiet chopping rhythm on clarinets over which we hear the most important theme of the movement. It is no more than a bare outline of G major.

Ex. 163

Individual brass instruments stand out in turn like heralds proclaiming this vital idea.

Now one of the most noticeable hall-marks of Stravinsky's style is what is called an *ostinato*—a continuous pattern of repetition in one part which goes on regardless of what may be happening elsewhere. Stravinsky will use such a pattern in two ways: either in direct repetition, or by ringing the changes on the *rhythm* while preserving the notes intact. Thus for twenty-three bars the 'cellos and basses pluck their way remorselessly through the three notes A C A.

Ex. 164

Above this systematic and regular pattern we find violent cross-'rhythms, syncopated splashes of piano chords, and a driving rhythmic urge which is a perfect reflection of modern industrial life. It is to such passages that the ballet sequences in a work like Leonard Bernstein's *West Side Story* owe their inception. As with

Picasso in the world of art, Stravinsky's influence on music extends into the most unlikely fields.

His second treatment of the *ostinato* pattern is shown in this example:

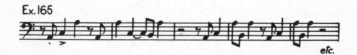

Ex. 165

etc.

The intrusion of the occasional B natural does not destroy the essential relationship that exists between this phrase and the preceding one. The basic A C A pattern continues like a carpet underfoot, its very consistency serving to heighten the extreme irregularity of the rhythms above. These are grouped in all sorts of variables of 3, 5, 11, 7, 4, and so on, so that the listener can never anticipate the duration of the next group. At last the *ostinato* releases its grip on the music, only to give way to a bass consisting entirely of segments of the scale of C major. It is interesting to see how Stravinsky's mind works when it comes to 'rethinking' the concept of a simple scale. The familiar outline of our schooldays is made considerably more exciting by this sort of treatment:

Ex. 166

etc.

Throughout this first movement an examination of the score shows how extraordinarily simple are the actual materials that Stravinsky uses. For bars on end the strings will have a brittle repetition of an ordinary G major arpeggio of three notes, while above, horns or trumpets will have sharp little outbursts built on conventional triads.[1] Yet despite this reliance on material from a

---

[1] A triad is the basic three-note chord of music, i.e., any note together with the third and the fifth above it. *Doh-mi-soh* is the simplest example.

first-year harmony book, Stravinsky's score sounds as searingly contemporary as any atonal work.

For development he draws mainly on the three-note pattern of Exx. 165 and 166. It appears both as a brief respite on quiet violas, and as a dry comment on the piano. The whole middle section of the movement is scored for altogether slenderer resources, and Stravinsky suggests something akin to a *concerto grosso* in the clearly defined contrasts of wind against strings, with the piano acting as a go-between. The writing is mostly contrapuntal in a free and fairly dissonant style, but the material is so clean-cut that the ear has no difficulty in disentangling one element from another. One important newcomer should be mentioned since much of the development section is based on it:

Ex.167

There are so many variants of this ascending scale that it is clearly Stravinsky's intention to develop the *idea* of a rising scale-pattern rather than any specific pattern itself. In fact, we can probably infer a relationship at least between these figures and Ex. 166.

Now it would be foolish to deny that at times Stravinsky's counterpoint is as thorny as a cactus; to ears brought up exclusively on a diet of what I once saw enchantingly described as 'Gilbert N. Sullivan', this score is virtually incomprehensible. However, once you are prepared to go out and meet Stravinsky and to see what his intentions are, you will inevitably find that this music is worth while. Not a note is wasted, and the elaborately spun texture of rhythms grows on one to such a point that in time the lush richness of a Brahms score will seem positively immoral in its hot-house sensuousness. A more detailed analysis of the first movement than I have attempted here would be uninformative and depressing—how else can I convey the arid boredom that comes from pointing out the obvious? Obvious would seem a strange word to use about a work such as this, but its structure is quite clearly defined, and the material easily recognizable. The main problem for the listener is to surrender his prejudices and to absorb the idiom. Unquestionably it is the sort of music where to follow a score is an enormous help; as with most of Stravinsky's works, a miniature score is available,[1] and any serious music-student should study it closely. Suffice it to say for the moment that the opening material returns in a conventional if somewhat abbreviated recapitulation, and that the movement ends with a quiet chorale-like coda that puts us in a suitable frame of mind for the Andante which follows.

This is in Stravinsky's favourite 'antique-restoring' idiom. The fascination with eighteenth-century music that seems to have been induced by *Pulcinella* stayed with him for a long time, and many of his works show him wrestling with the problem of endeavouring to re-create the delicacy and grace of Baroque[2] music in twentieth-century terms. The easy and non-productive way of doing this is to write attractive pieces called 'Dolly's Minuet' or 'The Dresden Shepherdess' and have them played in programmes for housewives; they will not be unduly concerned that you have produced something which is synthetic, plagiaristic, and Bad Art. To recapture the keenness of mind and the elegance of spirit of the Baroque composer is a different question; it means depriving oneself of all that the Romantic movement stands for, and making a conscious return to the stylistic purity of the truly classical composer. Stravinsky accomplishes this partly by using rhythms which we tend to associate with eighteenth-century music in particular (e.g. ♩♫♩.♩♫♩), and partly by a determination to eliminate what I might call the 'personal' element in composition. Classical music is objective, Romantic music is subjective; a return to Classicism involves the re-establishment of the barrier that Beethoven demolished, the barrier that made it seem improper

---

[1] Published by Schott, Ed. 4075.

[2] A somewhat loose term embracing a period of musical history of approximately 150 years from 1600 to 1750.

first-year harmony book, Stravinsky's score sounds as scaringly contemporary as any atonal work.

For development he draws mainly on the three-note pattern of Exx. 165 and 166. It appears both as a brief respite on quiet violas, and as a dry comment on the piano. The whole middle section of the movement is scored for altogether slenderer resources, and Stravinsky suggests something akin to a *concerto grosso* in the clearly defined contrasts of wind against strings, with the piano acting as a go-between. The writing is mostly contrapuntal in a free and fairly dissonant style, but the material is so clean-cut that the ear has no difficulty in disentangling one element from another. One important newcomer should be mentioned since much of the development section is based on it:

Ex.167

There are so many variants of this ascending scale that it is clearly Stravinsky's intention to develop the *idea* of a rising scale-pattern rather than any specific pattern itself. In fact, we can probably infer a relationship at least between these figures and Ex. 166.

Now it would be foolish to deny that at times Stravinsky's counterpoint is as thorny as a cactus; to ears brought up exclusively on a diet of what I once saw enchantingly described as 'Gilbert N. Sullivan', this score is virtually incomprehensible. However, once you are prepared to go out and meet Stravinsky and to see what his intentions are, you will inevitably find that this music is worth while. Not a note is wasted, and the elaborately spun texture of rhythms grows on one to such a point that in time the lush richness of a Brahms score will seem positively immoral in its hot-house sensuousness. A more detailed analysis of the first movement than I have attempted here would be uninformative and depressing—how else can I convey the arid boredom that comes from pointing out the obvious? Obvious would seem a

strange word to use about a work such as this, but its structure is
quite clearly defined, and the material easily recognizable. The
main problem for the listener is to surrender his prejudices and to
absorb the idiom. Unquestionably it is the sort of music where to
follow a score is an enormous help; as with most of Stravinsky's
works, a miniature score is available,[1] and any serious music-
student should study it closely. Suffice it to say for the moment
that the opening material returns in a conventional if somewhat
abbreviated recapitulation, and that the movement ends with a
quiet chorale-like coda that puts us in a suitable frame of mind for
the Andante which follows.

This is in Stravinsky's favourite 'antique-restoring' idiom. The
fascination with eighteenth-century music that seems to have been
induced by *Pulcinella* stayed with him for a long time, and many
of his works show him wrestling with the problem of endeavouring to re-create the delicacy and grace of Baroque[2] music in
twentieth-century terms. The easy and non-productive way of
doing this is to write attractive pieces called 'Dolly's Minuet' or
'The Dresden Shepherdess' and have them played in programmes
for housewives; they will not be unduly concerned that you have
produced something which is synthetic, plagiaristic, and Bad Art.
To recapture the keenness of mind and the elegance of spirit of
the Baroque composer is a different question; it means depriving
oneself of all that the Romantic movement stands for, and making
a conscious return to the stylistic purity of the truly classical
composer. Stravinsky accomplishes this partly by using rhythms
which we tend to associate with eighteenth-century music in
particular (e.g. ♩♫♫♩♫♫♩), and partly by a determination to
eliminate what I might call the 'personal' element in composition.
Classical music is objective, Romantic music is subjective; a return
to Classicism involves the re-establishment of the barrier that
Beethoven demolished, the barrier that made it seem improper

[1] Published by Schott, Ed. 4075.
[2] A somewhat loose term embracing a period of musical history of approximately
150 years from 1600 to 1750.

Ex.170

This barrack-room ballad has some pretty disturbing things going on underneath, and it would be misleading to suggest that we get an impression of C major unadulterated.

A brief quieter spell shows the bass clarinet trying on a seventh for size beneath a discreet murmur from the strings, and then we are off again on another display of explosive energy.

The indication 'piu presto' ushers in a somewhat disputatious dialogue between two bassoons which, despite its tensions, is conducted in decently muted tones. Other voices join in, and the listener is momentarily baffled by what seems like a confusion on Stravinsky's part as he introduces one fragment after another without seeming to show a particular affection for any one. In fact, he is again using the technique already mentioned on p. 145 by which he deals not with a theme but the *shape* of a theme. Everything here is concerned with three adjacent notes, and the next example shows several themes having this factor in common.

Ex.171

In such a way Stravinsky imposes a feeling of unity over fragments which at a first hearing seem to be unrelated. Gradually the music grows more positive until the horns give voice to a theme which recalls the folk-music of some of his early ballet scores.

Ex.172

The strings join in, in a similar vein, albeit with different material, until the whole orchestra starts to fidget with Ex. 171c. This section ends with some exciting screams from the horns. Propriety is restored by the bassoons who now present Ex. 170 in straight military costume in the typical march style that Stravinsky had so enjoyed in *L'Histoire du Soldat*. Everything seems to be going swimmingly when the triumphant course of the music is interrupted by some doleful sighs from the bassoons. These may be prompted by the sight of the academic task ahead, as though a Boy Scouts' hike had ended up with prep. in the classroom. Over the page there lurks a fugue.

The oboe had already made an unsuccessful attempt to think of the subject in Ex. 171a. Now it is presented in the unlikely colouring of trombone and piano, and although the various entries are by no means exact the theme is always identifiable, since it starts with an indeterminate rocking to and fro on two notes.

Ex.173

A curiously restless *agitato* section abbreviates this already concise subject still further:

Ex.174

Suddenly Stravinsky seems to lose patience with it all, and some strident chords in wind and piano blow it away. The movement ends in a dissonant blare of sound, its last chord a shattering denial of the C major from which the symphony had sprung. It is strong meat this, and demands a spirit of adventure from its audience; if you like the negative listening of the arm-chair addict it is not for you. Stravinsky takes you by a very firm grip and shouts his message in your ear; those who have taken the trouble to listen with understanding have found that he really has something to say.

INDEX

Abercrombie, Sir Ralph, 59
Allgemeine Musikalische Zeitung (quotation from), 70
Amens, 13, 98, 105
'Apotheosis of the Dance', 86
'Atonal', 22, 145
Atonal composers, 128

Bach, J. C., 38
Bach, J. S., 38, 76, 98, 141; his orchestration, 44; Brandenburg Concertos, 44; Suites, 44
Baroque music, 146, 147
Barrier of good taste, 147
Bartók, 58, 97
Battle of Alexandria, 59
Beddoes, Thomas Lovell, 104
Beethoven, 15, 23, 36, 43, 45, 96, 97, 98, 100, 102, 108, 119, 128, 129; Symphonies: No. 1, 71; No. 2, 50, 61, 71, 80, 86; No. 3, 'Eroica', Ch. IV; No. 4, 71; No. 5, 18, 46, 64, 78, 148; No. 6, 'Pastoral', 92, 100; No. 7, Ch. V, 60; ornaments in 2nd movement, 81; No. 9, 48, 71, 78; 'Battle' Symphony, 61; *Fidelio*, 50, 82; 4th Piano Concerto, 37, 38; Quartet Op. 127 in E♭, 49; last quartets, 94; *Prometheus* ballet-music, 66; *Prometheus* theme, 66, 69; Variations for Piano Op. 35, 66; Pathétique Sonata, 12, 72; Piano Sonata Op. 31 No. 2, 42 fn.; Piano Sonata Op. 109, 94; *Heiligenstadt Testament*, 50; conflicting tonalities investigated, 85; contemporary criticism, 70, 80 fn., 83; deafness, 49, 50; dynamic, changes of, 55, 76, 79; Haydn's

influence, 86; humour, 67, 77; master of prepared surprise, 80; own words, 75 fn., 89, 92 fn.; Scherzo form, 61, 86; sense of architecture, 71, 72, 86; sketches, 51, 52, 62, 65; tempo changes in later works, 94; tonal balance, 85; unexpected key changes, 58, 74, 79, 83–5; use of silence, 67, 68, 78; Variation form, 66–70; violent change of mood, 83
Berg, 128
Berlioz, *Symphonie Fantastique*, Ch. VI; *Lélio*, 92; *Les Francs-Juges*, 101; Autobiography, 93; dramatic quality, 103; ear for colour, 102; feelings for Harriet Smithson, 93; *Idée fixe*, 94; influenced by Beethoven, 100; melodic treatment, 95, 100; orchestration, 92, 94, 97, 98, 99, 101, 102, 103, 131; originality, 96, 97, 103; reason for use of literary programme, 93; revelling in sonority, 94; special indications on score, 90, 97, 103, 105, 106; use of intricate rhythms, 100; violent dynamics, 94, 106
Bernadotte, General, 50
Bernstein, Leonard, 144
Blenheim Palace, 11
'Bluebells of Scotland, The', 10, 20
Böhm, 49, 50
Bottom (*Midsummer Night's Dream*), 121
Brahms, 16, 36, 128, 129, 145; Symphony No. 1, 108, 109; No. 2, Ch. VII, 109, 130; Piano Concerto No. 2 in B♭, 125; Violin Sonata in A Op. 100, 120 fn.;